GOLD, FRANKINCENSE, & MYRRH

by

Ralph Adams Cram

Bona Tempora Volvant

Arcadia
MMXVIII

Printed in the United States of America

ISBN 978-1-944339-12-8

Gold, Frankincense, & Myrrh

Published by Tumblar House
Visit our website at www.tumblarhouse.com

TABLE OF CONTENTS

FOREWORD 1
PREFACE 8
MONASTICISM AND THE WORLD CRISIS 10
SACRAMENTALISM AND THE FUTURE 32
THE PHILOSOPHICAL NECESSITY 54

FOREWORD

Charles A. Coulombe

THE PERIOD OF AMERICAN HISTORY that most defined these United States was that from 1865 to 1941. Before those years, we were a collection of semi-independent sovereign States; afterwards we were (and are) an empire dedicated to imposing an ever-changing notion of "freedom" over a world that is by turns accepting and resistant—depending upon what and where we are peddling. But during that period, our national identity gelled. The current methods of celebrating our national calendar of holidays—Labor Day, Halloween, Veterans Day, Thanksgiving, Christmas, Lincoln's and Washington's Birthdays, Easter, Decoration/Memorial Day, Independence Day, Flag Day, and the rest—developed. Vaudeville, Broadway, Hollywood, and at last radio not only successively entertained but defined America to its inhabitants and the rest of humanity, and the Indian-haunted frontier made way for the National Park System. Cocktails (despite and perhaps because of Prohibition) and canning dominated our drink—and foodways, while Irving Berlin and Norman Rockwell provided sight and sound. From Mark Twain to Fitzgerald and Hemingway, the broad corpus of American literature was being written, as was the Great American Songbook. All the while this was going on, Americans were founding organisations that influence us to this day: the Daughters of the American Revolution,

YMCA, Knights of Columbus, American Legion, Elks, Boy Scouts, and dozens of others. Waves of immigration brought the majority of our non-Indian, Black, and WASP forebears here.

While all of this self-creation was going on in so many areas, nowhere was it more evident than in architecture and landscape. Frederick Law Olmsted and the City Beautiful Movement were creating the parks and urban monuments that dominate many of our cities and towns even today, while such as Frank Lloyd Wright were having a huge impact on house design. But one name stands foremost in architecture during this era: Ralph Adams Cram (1863-1942).

Although Cram and his still existing firm of Cram and Ferguson designed and continue to design a wide variety of private and public buildings, it was primarily in collegiate and ecclesiastical architecture that they have left their broad mark on the American landscape. In the former sphere, West Point, Princeton, Rollins College, Rice University, USC, and a number of other such institutions all feature Cram's work. But it was for churches that Cram was primarily known, in most major cities and a number of smaller towns, stretching from Boston's All Saints, Ashmont and New York's Cathedral of St. John the Divine and St. Thomas Church to St. Vincent's in Los Angeles and Central Congregational Church in Honolulu. Although comfortable working in such diverse styles as Spanish Baroque and Japanese, it was his distinctly American style of Neo-Gothic for which he is most famous. It is not too much to say that he created the defining look for colleges and churches that still dominates the American popular imagination to this day.

Were that his only achievement, Ralph Adams Cram would be worthy of our attention. But it is not. Although born to a Unitarian Minister in New Hampshire and raised in that quintessentially American faith, a youthful visit to Rome converted him to what he considered Catholicism—in this case, that variant of the Anglican faith called Anglo-Catholicism. Created in 1830s England by the Oxford Movement (headed by John Henry Newman, who would later convert to Rome, and Edward Pusey, who would not), Anglo-Catholicism had a huge influence on the Church of England and its daughter churches, including the Episcopal Church in the United States, which Cram joined on his return to America. The Anglo-Catholics brought back to Anglicanism such beliefs and practises banished by the Reformation or the English Civil War as devotion to the Blessed Sacrament, the Virgin Mary, and the Saints; prayers for the dead; and monasticism for both men and women. They conceived of themselves as having the mission of "re-Catholicising" the Anglican Communion: for all, this meant seeing Anglicanism as a "branch" of the One True Church, alongside Roman Catholicism and Eastern Orthodoxy; for many (including Cram), this also meant working for eventual corporate reunion with Rome.

This creed also had political implications. For one thing, it meant the revival of the *cultus* of King Charles I, the only individual Anglicanism ever attempted to canonise: he was seen as a martyr, since Cromwell and his confederates would have spared the King's life had he been willing to sign off on the abolition of Bishops in the Church of England (others noted as well that his intermittent negations with the Holy See were another reason for his judicial murder). This in turn led some English Anglo-Catholics (and some Romans there as well) to revive interest in Jacobitism and the House of Stuart, which resulted in the formation of groups such as the Order of the White Rose (forerunner of today's Royal Stuart Society). It also led to opposition to industrialism and monopoly capitalism along the lines of Catholic thinking in Continental Europe and Latin America—and the emergence of such thinkers as G.K. Chesterton and Arthur Penty, who looked to Medieval Christendom for inspiration in building a new social and economic order: this duo would enter the Catholic Church under the aegis of Hilaire Belloc. For American proponents of these views, it also led to a renewed consciousness of the United States as integral parts of the Anglosphere, alongside Great Britain, Ireland, Canada, Australia, New Zealand, and South Africa.

Cram drank deeply of these religious and political views. A devotee of the liturgical and devotional practises revived by Anglo-Catholicism, he was also a co-founder of the American branches of the Society of King Charles the Martyr and the Order of the White Rose (both of which met in what is now Boston's Isabella Stewart Gardner Museum). Cram was instrumental in bringing the Anglican Cowley Fathers to America, even designing their still-existing monastery outside Boston. An avid traveller in Britain and Europe, he came to know Belloc, Chesterton, and Penty well. No doubt influenced by his interaction with them, he became involved with a number of Roman Catholic enterprises in the United States—going so far as to co-found *Commonweal* (though what he would think of it now is anyone's guess).

But beyond all that, Cram left us a large number of works on political and social issues, to which the one before you—*Gold, Frankincense, and Myrrh*—is a splendid introduction. Not bothering with our national superstitions regarding Church and State, he points out that America needs what any Christian society needs to survive and thrive—a Sacramental view of life, Monasticism, and proper philosophy. He would enlarge upon these views in such works written before and after this one as *The Great Thousand Years*, *Towards the Great Peace*, and *The End of Democracy*, as well as articles in such journals as *The American Review* and *The American Mercury*. As he shows repeatedly, we Americans—for all of our uniqueness—are not immune to the laws of history, human nature, and indeed, the religious requirements of God. If we are to survive, we must somehow accommodate our system—based as it is on very different premises—to these realities.

All that being true, one might well wonder why his work, so long out of print, is important to us now. Partly, it is because the issues he raises and attempts to offer some reply to are still very much with us, and it were well if we examined the work of a man who saw so much so clearly. Partly because, alongside the work of such as C.S. Lewis, Charles Williams, T.S. Eliot, Arthur Machen, and others, Cram's legacy is part of that Anglican Patrimony which Benedict XVI created the Personal Ordinariates within the Catholic Church to preserve, and which he described as "a precious gift nourishing the faith of the members of the Ordinariate and as a treasure to be shared."

A last question that might well be asked is that if Cram saw things so clearly, accepted Papal primacy, and so often defended the Church against anti-Catholic prejudice, why did he not convert himself? The answer is to be found in the enormous success of the Anglo-Catholic movement in his lifetime (and to which he mightily contributed). The huge Anglo-Catholic Congresses and pilgrimages during the interwar years and the multiplication of such Anglican religious communities as the Cowley and Mirfield Fathers and the Nashdom Benedictines across the British Empire and the United States seemed to indicate that the Anglo-Catholic Movement would succeed, and that a Catholicised Anglican Communion would seek corporate reunion with the Holy See in the relatively near future. He could not have foreseen what would happen after his death.

What did happen—the collapse not merely of Anglo-Catholicism but even of "mere Christianity" within the Anglican Communion—has been an agony that he was spared. Inevitable as it seems now, given Anglicanism's ecclesiological nature, it has nevertheless been a tragedy to watch for those who love the English-speaking culture with which it has been so bound up. That tragedy is in many ways connected with the self-inflicted implosion that has struck the Catholic Church and Western culture as a whole in at least the past six decades. But the creation of the Ordinariates gives hope that whatever was worthwhile in the Anglican Patrimony—not least Cram's literary and architectural legacy—shall survive within the Church, and help stimulate her revival and a true "New Evangelisation" in the Anglosphere. If he is in a position to enjoy it, the fact that the American Ordinariate's recently-built cathedral in

Houston was designed by his old firm of Cram and Ferguson must be a source of intense joy to him. Certainly, as with the rest of Cram's legacy, it can be to all who those fortunate enough to enjoy it.

    Charles A. Coulombe
    Monrovia, CA
    Feast of Ss. Cyriacus, Largus, and Smaragdus
    August 8, 2018

PREFACE

OF THE THREE ADDRESSES that make up this volume, the first was delivered in 1917 before the students of the General Theological Seminary in New York, the second at the fiftieth anniversary of the Confraternity of the Blessed Sacrament, at the Church of St. Mary the Virgin in New York, in 1918, while the third was read at a meeting of the Clerical Brotherhood of the Episcopal Church in the Diocese of Pennsylvania, at Philadelphia, in 1919. All three have been published in *The American Church Monthly*, and permission to reprint has been given by the editor, the Reverend Selden Peabody Delany, D.D. The third of the addresses, "The Philosophical Necessity," has also been republished by the Reverend Thomas Edward Shields, D.D., in *The Catholic Educational Review*.

For the doctrines, statements and inferences that are to be found in the three addresses, no responsibility can in any degree be attached to the governing body of the General Theological Seminary or to the officers of the Confraternity of the Blessed Sacrament or to the Bishop of Pennsylvania. The various papers were read without having been first given a *nihil obstat* by any one in authority, and I desire to take entirely on my own shoulders the responsibility for what I have said. As the third essay is in a sense an extension and amplification of the second, and as it was given before a different audience, certain repetitions occur, but it has seemed best to leave the papers in their original estate, except that from the second has been omitted the philosophical argument for the doctrine of Transubstantiation (this also was left out in *The American Church Monthly*) which was later amplified into the Philadelphia address.

The title "Gold, Frankincense and Myrrh" means simply this: Gold is the pure, imperishable quality of the monastic ideal, Frankincense the supreme act of worship through the Blessed Sacrament, Myrrh the saving quality of a right philosophy of life that yet must be bitter to the taste of many people. Together they are the three gifts that must again be offered by a world once more led, though now by the red and malefic star of war, to worship and fall down before the Incarnate God so long and so lightly denied.

RALPH ADAMS CRAM.
23rd June, 1919.

MONASTICISM AND THE WORLD CRISIS

LIKE ALL THE MANIFESTATIONS of natural forces, like the pulsing of the lifeblood, like life itself, history is a system of vast vibrations, systole and diastole beating eternally, but with nodes that are separated not by fractional seconds, but by intervals of five centuries. From the day of the Incarnation, back through Europe, Asia, Africa, until chronology merges in myth and tradition, and on, even to this day, and so forward until the end, this enormous vibration controls and conditions man, and he plays his part on the rise, the crest, or the descent of the wave, helpless to change its course or to avert its fall.

The fable of evolution, the delusion of continuous progress, the dream of the final perfectibility of man on earth, break down and die under the hard light of universal catastrophe, vanishing with all the other illusions of modernism that have made that catastrophe not a ghastly accident but an expiation and a potential redemption, while blinding the world to its implacable approach. For the individual there may be progress, but the rise from birth to maturity is followed by declension to the grave. For the community or the state there may be progress, but the

Monasticism and the World Crisis 11

upward sweep of the *élan vital*[1] curves at last, in its brief trajectory, to merge again in the inert mass through which it sprang, and the jungles of Asia, the sands of African deserts, the forests of Europe hide the forgotten shards of universal civilizations whose names are words only, and whose deeds are of the dust that buries their monuments. For mankind itself there may be progress, out of periodical misery and oblivion, upward to honor and dignity and worth and power, but always the parabola traces its dying fall, and this spurt of progress lasts not five centuries, beyond which term nothing may pass without failure, extinction and supersession.

History is a series of resurrections, for the rhythm of change is invariable. Each epoch of five hundred years follows the same monotonous course, though made distinctive by new variations. Since the Christian era Imperial Rome has risen, culminated and disappeared "under the drums and tramplings of four conquests." The Eastern Empire has succeeded, with the first congeries of Christian states in the West. Mediævalism has burst like a new day on Europe, to go to its end five centuries later as our own epoch began its astounding career. The birth of Christ, the years 500, 1000, 1500, are nodal points when all that had been ceased and new things came into being: before the year 2000, now but two generations away, modern civilization will have passed and a new era have taken its place. Already the whirlwind of destruction has

---

[1] *élan vital* - the vital force or impulse of life; especially: a creative principle held by Bergson to be immanent in all organisms and responsible for evolution.

overtaken it, and for more than three years, it has suffered the first of the assaults that will in the end make it one with Babylon and with Nineveh.

We are today in the midst of just such a grinding collapse as that which overtook Rome and the empire of Charlemagne and the Christian Commonwealths of the Middle Ages, and we shall escape no more than they. Neither scientific accomplishment nor efficiency, neither parliamentary government nor industrialism, neither wealth nor self-confidence, neither pacifism nor neutrality can save us, for we have reached the crest of folly that crowns achievement, and beyond lies the shuddering fall into the trough of the heaving sea. But the wave, if it falls, rises again, and history, if it shouts its warning, whispers also its hope. If night follows day, day follows night, and since Christ came we have not only the hope but the way. And the way has never changed in essence, though it has varied widely in its manifestations. As Rome fell, St. Benedict of Nursia rose above the welter of ruin to save what might be saved and to build society anew. As the first Holy Roman Empire broke down in ruin, St. Odo of Cluny in his turn saved something from the wreck, began the new era of Christian civilization in the North, and gave it to St. Robert of Molesmes, who transformed it by Cistercianism into a thing of unexampled nobility and fixed forever the standard type of Christian society. When at last this also began to decline, its time having arrived, a sudden new life swept through the moribund orders, —Benedictine, Cistercian, Dominican, —making them once more constructive and regenerative agencies, while by means of an entirely novel version of the monastic method, St. Ignatius Loyola stopped the progress of devouring heresy and concentrated in centers of tremendous dynamic force the shattered and dislocated elements of Catholic Christianity, that they might engender the counter-reformation and preserve fundamental Christianity until better days.

So in the first years of the sixth century, the last years of the tenth, and the first years of the sixteenth, at intervals of approximately five hundred years, just at the nodal point where one era was dying in dishonor, and another rising in power, came a new outpouring of monastic fervor to save and to recreate. In the year 927 St. Odo promulgated the reformed rule of the Order of Cluny, and the Dark Ages came to an end within sixty years, to give place to Christian civilization. One thousand years from then will bring us to the year 1927, but we need not wait until then for the assurance that God has again been merciful and given the world a new hope, for nearly fifty years ago came the first evidences of the new life, and now the death of civilization seals the early assurance, and everywhere may be seen the stirrings of the Holy Spirit leading men once more into this earthly army of God.

For it is the consecrated Religious Life that has been the divine agency for the saving of the world at all its moments of most critical peril; and if you will study the phenomena of periodic degeneration, and the spirit and method of monasticism, you will see that this must inevitably be so. As each era of the world reaches its fulfillment, it suddenly festers into five cancerous sores: wealth and luxury, lust and licentiousness, wilfulness and individualism, leading in the end to anarchy, envy and egotism, and finally the idleness of the parasite. You will find most of these, in varying measure, in the last years of Rome, of the Carolingian Empire and the Eastern Empire, of the epoch of Mediævalism; and you will find them all, and without measure, in the last years of the nineteenth and the elapsed years of the twentieth century.

Now against them the Religious Life has set the three great evangelical councils of Poverty, Chastity and Obedience, adding to them two other principles of equal value, viz., Brotherhood and Work. Each is the explicit negation and corrective of some one of the sins of success, and together they form the energizing force that brings a new era into being.

There is no other way. As an era dies, it engenders an all-embracing mortality in its members, and there is nothing essentially of itself, either in its works or its men, that retains regenerative power. When an age dies, it dies altogether, though such spiritual force as it may have generated continues beyond its own decadence and fall as a slowly dissipating impulse in art. In the end this is dispersed and art ceases for the time, but it never had a truly vital quality in the establishing and determining of spiritual values, finding its function only in an empty aestheticism that ended at last in the various historical predecessors of *art nouveau* and *vers libre*. As in all life, the dynamic impulse towards new things comes from without, a sudden jet of the *élan vital*, expressing itself through a swift intensification—exaggeration if you like—of those fundamental principles of all wholesome society that have been lost out of life and must in some way be restored.

It is not necessary to maintain that the monastic life is an universal ideal: the claim is not even made. It is rather a highly special form of life, normally fitted for comparatively few men and women; but at abnormal times, such as the closing years of an epoch, it becomes not a refuge but a duty and a call to sacrifice. The army is not the normal life for all, but at critical moments, when honor and justice and eternal truths are imperiled, it sends its clear call to all men for holy service in warfare. Nothing can take its place; none of the agencies of peace and order may serve; and if men do not arise, and at any cost, even of life itself, range themselves in the front of battle, nothing follows but humiliation, disaster, and the death of more than men and women and children.

The Religious Life is a life of continual sacrifice, but nothing of enduring value in the world has been attained except through sacrifice. Wealth and ease, peace and plenty, material success and serene content, never won anything, either for the individual, the community or the state, while they lead inevitably to decadence and downfall. Adversity and suffering, sorrow and labor and sacrifice, are the builders of character, the foundation-stones of righteous civilization. Out of these sacrifices that monasticism demands, has come for myriads of men and women more than adequate personal compensation, as this comes to the soldier in the trenches of France, dying a clean death in a holy cause. This, however, is only a by-product; the great thing is the unique and splendid opportunity for service, for the doing of what no one else can do, and this the noblest service that man can render to man. For more than two years millions of men and boys have sacrificed all that life could give to save something from the wreck of a world, and their sacrifice will not be in vain so far as the first victory at arms is concerned. It will, in the end, have been in vain if there are not now the few thousands of their brothers to make their smaller sacrifice in order that the victory they have bought with their blood may be sealed by that spiritual regeneration which always has been, and always will be, the work of those whom God has called to the Religious Life.

As we look back through history we can see how terrible was the fall, how gross the enveloping darkness of the end of Antiquity, of the close of the Dark Ages, of the break-up of Mediævalism. We cannot imagine what fearful fate must have over-taken the world if it had not been for the followers of the consecrated Religious Life, from St. Benedict to St. Ignatius Loyola. Today the fall and the darkness are more profound than ever before, except possibly at the end of the Roman Empire; therefore the old call is more insistent as the need is correspondingly greater. Everything with which and by which our modern era has lived, shatters before us, and no visible foundation remains. Protestantism and free thought, parliamentary government and democracy, natural science, industrial civilization and material efficiency, evolutionary philosophy, pragmatism, determinism, freedom of speech and freedom of the press and compulsory public education—all these, and their myriad concomitants, crumble, totter, and melt away before the Frankenstein monster they themselves had created.

I do not mean that all these proud products of modernism now show themselves as entirely empty delusions, for the greater part of them express some element of truth or usefulness. In every case, however, they have either been exaggerated out of all reason, falsified by removal from contact with some other opposed principle which alone could have acted as a corrective, or finally their original idea has been lost sight of under some mechanistic incubus we have invented as a means to an end, and then have accepted as the end in itself, to the utter forgetfulness of the object of our labor, which has consequently disappeared. An example of what I mean is democracy, which is a splendid ideal in itself, and worth fighting for; but for a century we have been so ridiculously busy in inventing new engines for creating it, in discovering new panaceas for correcting our interminable failures, that at last we have not the remotest idea in what democracy consists, and actually, in the midst of an insane phantasmagoria of political devices, have seen not only the humiliating failure of these patented nostrums but the almost complete disappearance of the democratic idea as a moving cause or even as a dim and mythical tradition.

So it is with the other things I have named, and as they break down visibly before us, we realize that the very foundations of life are overturned, that our light has become darkness, and we have no guide for our steps. We have made our world over to suit ourselves, and at the very moment when we look on it and see that it is good, it crumbles into mere debris; hollow, unsubstantial, insecure, it cannot endure the touch of real life, and breaks in pieces of its own unwieldiness.

In all this there is no ground for final discouragement. All depends on how we meet the crisis, how we bear the test, with what standards we measure the new, hard, and even appalling things that are put before us. At last Calvinism is no longer upon us, to weigh us down under a base fatalism. We know our choice is free, and we may will a new Dark Ages or a new Renaissance—better still a new Mediævalism. All depends on how we, ourselves, meet the issue.

For this vast cataclysm is not a trying out of individuals, or of a few nations, but of all men, east, west, north and south. None may escape, for, each in its own degree, every race on earth lies under the same condemnation, from Russia, which had surrendered least, to Prussia, which had surrendered all. A system nearly five centuries old is being tried that it may be destroyed, and destroyed that something better may take its place.

As five centuries ago, and ten and fifteen and twenty, the saving motive will be the Catholic Faith, poured out anew upon the nations; and as five centuries ago, and ten and fifteen, the visible and divinely directed means will be the consecrated Religious Life. Not through archaic and pictorial revivals, but under the drive of a new spiritual consciousness implanted in man by God the Holy Ghost, working itself out under old rules and under reformed rules, but in essence what it always has been and always will be. Monasticism—I use the term generally as including all types of monks, friars, canons-regular, and missionaries bound under the vows of poverty, chastity, and obedience—is divine in its essence and its order, therefore an essential and indestructible portion of the visible Catholic Church, but it is manifested through human agencies, therefore fallible and destined to decay and to demand reform; destined equally to adapt itself to new times and to new conditions. Within these great and closing walls of poverty, chastity and obedience, brotherhood and work, it

Monasticism and the World Crisis

will transmute itself into new forms, but always there will be three great classes, the general motive of which will never change, and the demand for which, and for all, was never more insistent than today; and these three are the monk, the friar and the canon-regular. Let me try to show why each is needed today, whether he lives under the old rules of St. Benedict, St. Francis or St. Augustine, or under some modification thereof.

The ideal of the true monk is furthest from the spirit of today—or rather of yesterday. There *is* no "today," but only an interlude of anarchy, and the monk is therefore more essential at this crisis than the friar or the canon-regular, however imperative may be the demand for both, and the demand is insistent and clamorous. The friar and the canon-regular are the workers of visible things, and a world of efficiency and "the strenuous life," whose gospel is "get results," can measurably understand them. The monk, cloistered, shut away from active contact with the world, living a life of rigid abstinence, praying, praising God and giving himself over to intercession, adoration and worship, is to the world unthinkable, but it is at times like this that the world needs him most. Action—feverish, insistent, universal—has built up a world that has failed, and out of that failure will come the consciousness that the real things in life are of the spirit, not of the flesh, not of man but of God. Great and glorious works have come from the labors of men, whether they were Religious or seculars or laymen, but the greatest things came, not from their physical action but from their spiritual energy; and though with their hands they have built up great fabrics of civilization and given them life through the energy of ordered intellects, the soul of these civilizations came as the gift of God, through His saints, and because of the prayers and intercessions and the worship of His children. The monk who made a desert into a garden, or turned a heathen people from savagery, did well, but he did better when prostrating himself in prayer in the silence of his cell, or when he joined with his brethren in beseeching Our Lady and the saints for their intercessions, or in worshiping the incarnate God in the Holy Sacrament of the Altar.

Our age is dying because it has lost *spiritual* energy, and therefore no longer knows the difference between the real and the false, the temporal and the eternal, between right and wrong, and this spiritual energy is to be restored, not by action, but by the grace of God, —and by prayer alone is this grace given to men. We need the spiritual energy that emanates from the hushed cloisters and the dim chapels of brotherhoods of monks, and the invincible force of their intercessions. If only we knew that here and there, hidden in the still country-side, the sons of St. Benedict, as they were in the sixth century and the eleventh, were fighting, day and night, the spiritual battle that is more arduous even than the physical, we could take heart of hope where now is opportunity for little but despair.

Thus far, with us, scant progress has been made towards the restoration of a strict monasticism, all our new orders having been formed along the lines of communities of canons-regular or friars. Caldey tried it, and poor Father Ignatius even earlier, but *Ecclesia Anglicana* had no place for that sort of thing and Caldey was forced, by the logic of consistency, to make its submission to Rome. Even there too much time was given to preaching far afield, and to other extraneous objects, just as, under the Roman obedience, the Benedictine houses have largely forsaken their ordained work, in the interests of schools and missions, and even the cure of souls. The spirit of strict monasticism seems almost wholly to have died away, and because of this the present peril of the world is increased. Unless it can be restored, now, without loss of time, the immediate future can give little hope. Unfortunately to few is given the monastic vocation, and when it is vouchsafed, only too often the doubtful listener closes his ears, thinking, under the black inheritance of strenuousness, that action alone will "get results," and that he has no right to remain outside the ranks of those who are everlastingly "up and doing." For the restoration of a clearer sense of spiritual values we must insistently pray, and if the world is to be saved from an era of the Dark Ages, sooner or later our prayer will be answered.

Strictly speaking, the orders of preaching friars have not been restored with us as yet. Rome has done better there than with the monks, the Dominicans having not only preserved their fine tradition, but of late acquired a new fire and fervor that have made them a great vitalizing power. In England the Society of the Divine Compassion is a genuinely Franciscan foundation, and we once had here, in Father Paul, a possible center for a similar work. He has now accepted Roman jurisdiction and is finding there the support of men and the charity denied him in his earlier days, so all this must be done over again, perhaps now, under the conditions of the present *débâcle*, with better chance of success.

The importance to us of an immediate restoration of the two chief orders, Franciscan and Dominican, cannot be overestimated. Our fat and futile social organism, where wealth is the chief stimulus to action, and the first consideration in political, industrial and social affairs, —the great substitution of modernism for honor, courage and duty, — must be met by the consecrated poverty of the Franciscan, fearlessly denouncing a condition of things that, when civilization returns again, will be bracketed in later histories with the epochs in the Dark Ages and during the Renaissance when simony had rotted the Church and society to a point wherefrom recovery was possible only by the direct intervention of God. In our economic-industrial state we are confronted by a steady progress away from the free association of the Middle Ages, back to the "Servile State" of antiquity, with the certainty that before this is accomplished there will be war that is overt, bloody and relentless. If we are to escape this I believe it can only be through the intervention of the poor brothers of St. Francis, glorifying poverty, love and labor over and above the principles that are now the guiding stars of our decline.

And what of the Dominicans? Surely, if ever, we need now their fearless and insistent defense of Catholic truth. It is a custom to call ourselves a Christian nation, just as before the war we spoke of the "Christian civilization" of Europe. It is also customary for some of us to speak of the Episcopal Church as a Catholic Church. If we speak from a lively faith our convictions do us honor, as must all faith that relies on an inner conviction, not on apparent facts. In any case we are compelled to admit that less than half the people, of America even, call themselves Christians of one sort or another, and that there is enough unblushing heresy high in honor within the Anglican Church to bring it to shipwreck unless it meets with vigorous counteraction. Neither St. Athanasius nor St. Dominic nor St. Ignatius Loyola ever confronted bolder and more insidious unfaith and disloyalty. Just because more and more Presbyterians build Gothic churches, with stained-glass windows and twenty thousand dollar organs, and an increasing number of our clergy wear Eucharistic vestments and put two candles (frequently unlighted) on their altars, we think that all is well.

Strong defense of the Catholic Faith and nothing but the Catholic Faith, asserted openly, everywhere and insistently, is a crying need of our time, and without this every effort at a redemption of society will fail, unless we are willing to count alone on the "uncovenanted mercies of God." There will be no new and better day for the world unless underneath and interpenetrating present life and the social fabric is the definite, dogmatic, and sacramental religion that has made and preserved the Catholic Church and Christian society from the day of Pentecost. Give us once more the Order of Preachers of St. Dominic, bound under the threefold rule, with no parochial obligations, but going far and wide, in poverty and in the willingness for martyrdom if necessary, and we shall not have to ask so much of some of our bishops and our parish clergy who already are crushed under the weight of their special duties.

The third class, that of the canons-regular, really comprises the greater part of our Religious Orders today, at the head standing the Society of St. John the Evangelist. Mission priests they truly are, and this function is equal in importance with the others I have named. I say less of them now, for we know them better, and no word is necessary to justify them or to add to the demand that their numbers should be increased. I think, however, there is a very real demand that out of them should grow, and immediately, something more closely resembling the canons-regular of St. Augustine or those of St. Norbert. There should be, under every bishop, a kind of diocesan monastery, self-governing and self-contained, but subject to the call of the bishop for such service as he might demand, such as evangelical work in heathen districts, temporary charge of missions, emergency service in parishes, and the maintenance of church services and parish work where a certain minimum stipend could not be raised. Such houses of canons should receive young priests immediately after ordination, giving them work "under service conditions," on three-year and renewable vows, and also superannuated clergy who would form a nucleus of permanency. If possible, young men should be trained here for the priesthood, and small schools of orphan boys might be maintained. Within its precincts the house would be self-governing, with the bishop as visitor; but when a man was called out for active service, he would become the bishop's man, owing for the time obedience to him alone. Of course, there would be some arrangement whereby a certain number of men would always be left in the house for the conduct of its services and internal affairs, while no man should be compelled to absent himself except for a definite number of days at a time, during which period the bishop would be responsible for his maintenance. Every bishop would welcome such an engine of service as these diocesan monasteries would prove, and they seem the easiest of accomplishment, since normally their vows would be for short periods, and a clear vocation to the Religious Life— the hardest thing to find or to be sure of—would be less necessary than in the case of monks and friars. In a way each house of this kind would be a place for the discovering and testing of vocations, and while many would return to the secular priesthood, others would proceed to the contemplative or the active life of the Benedictine or Dominican or Franciscan rules.

Of these three definite systems, one must then immediately be widely strengthened and extended, the other two re-created. In the beginning the Benedictine, Franciscan, and Dominican rules should be accepted practically in their integrity. Experience will indicate necessary changes of adaptation, but there is none now who seems to possess that clear vision that would make possible either a new rule or the series of modifications of an old one that would perfectly meet the anomalous conditions of our time. Moreover, there is in monasticism something akin to the Apostolical Succession which alone guarantees a valid priesthood, and this identity of motive and continuity of tradition must be preserved. Every Religious since the sixth century has traced his lineage and his "mission" back to St. Benedict, and so it must always be. Gathered together under his patronage, and that of his successors, clear direction will be given as to the lines along which the necessary modification must proceed.

One may admit, and frankly, that the obstacles that stand in the way of this restoration and revival seem almost insuperable. They are not this, but only stimulating to a degree. Hitherto, when the need arose, some one man came forward, out of oblivion, to stir the world and gather together the necessary soldiers in God's new army. St Benedict, St. Berno, St. Robert of Molesmes, St. Stephen Harding, Chrodegang of Metz, St. Bernard, St. Bruno, St. Francis, St. Dominic, St. Ignatius Loyola, all were sudden and shining lights, vivid and dominant personalities filled with the Spirit of God, who had the vision, the power to interpret it, and the faculty of inspiring and leading men; and the same is true down even to our own day, in the persons of Father Benson, and Dom Aelred Carlyle, and Father Huntington. Under them the task was easy of accomplishment, but now we confront a new situation where there are no precedents to guide us. The War is a great wonder and prolific of many revelations, but none is more staggering than this: that now, at a moment when the world cries aloud for leadership as never before, there is none to answer. In no land, among no people, in no category of life, is there to be found today one leader of the first class; not a statesman, not a philosopher, hardly even a soldier, and with the exception of the Cardinal of Malines and certain of the French bishops, not a Churchman of the first class, to see, to interpret, to arouse or to lead. In these latter days modernism—largely through its basic principles of Protestantism, secularism and democracy—has reduced all men to a dead level of inferiority, from which no heroic leader lifts his head.

In some way, then, we must find a substitute for the great creators of Christian monasticism, since modern civilization has reached a point where leaders are no longer produced. The dangers that follow from this lack of leadership are deep-seated and sinister. Father Benson used to say that he had known few men with a vocation to be monks, but many with a vocation to be Fathers Superior. The danger of mistaken leadership, or of joint action without leadership, are very great. It takes several years to test a vocation, and many years to make a monk. Obedience is even a harder rule to follow than either poverty or chastity, and training is as necessary for a monk or friar as for an engineer or a physician. I see no alternative but for the tested Orders we have, such as the S.S.J.E. and Holy Cross, largely to abandon their other work in order that they may receive into their novitiates the men who may be drawn towards the Religious Life, to test and train them even for other houses and other possible Rules than their own. Could they do this, could they make this sacrifice, they might become the nurseries of a complete and saving system of monasticism. Another possibility would be the organization of the diocesan monasteries of canons-regular of which I have spoken, the prior in each case being at first novice-master as well, and a trained Religious loaned for a few years for this particular work. One warning cannot be too often reiterated, which is that the certain road to failure lies through a group of earnest and zealous men banding together to form a religious community, without disciplinary experience, and intent only on creating a center of monastic life out of their own inner consciousness. We have had rather too much of this of late, and the experiment must not be repeated.

So, then, we must begin by strengthening the S.S.J.E. and Holy Cross and at the same time restoring true monasticism through a revived Benedictinism, and the orders of

Franciscan and Dominican preaching friars. I am increasingly convinced that the work will not and must not stop here. The old rules must be amended and developed for new orders, but the time has come for a further extension of the monastic idea. In the beginning, in the time of Pachomius and the hermits of the desert, the unit was the individual, wholly withdrawn from the world and isolated in his mountain cave, or on the top of his column if his taste led in that direction. St. Benedict increased this unit through exalting the idea of human fellowship, and thereafter it consisted of groups, either of men or women, forming a centralized community. Then St. Ignatius Loyola increased the size of these groups, giving them the centralized control of an army. Now the time has come for a further extension of the great idea, not to the exclusion of the monastic unit or of the individual unit, but to supplement them. This new unit will be the family, men, women and children, in that most holy unit of all which is the Christian family, gathering together in places withdrawn from the world (as the world is now, and has been for nearly five centuries), where they can build up what I like to call "walled towns," —no more of the world than is the monastery, but like that constituted on lines of order, simplicity and righteousness. The headlong development of modernism has at last resulted in a social organism which is identical in all parts of the world and apparently invincible and irreformable—at all events of its own motion or from within. In the current effort of one section of this organism to establish by force and the denial of the last traces of an earlier Christian society its hegemony of the globe, the whole thing may be destroyed, as completely as Antiquity was destroyed, and

Monasticism and the World Crisis

before the end of the century we may be eking out a precarious and savage existence amid the crumbling ruins of a proud civilization that has passed away. The chances are that this is the fate in store for the world, which is very given to "vain repetitions"; but if for the moment this catastrophe is delayed, as Rome sporadically revived in a measure, and with failing vigor, between the successive barbarian invasions, then the immediate question will be, What course are they to pursue who have read the writing on the wall and have seen the present phantasm of culture only as a silly mockery, incapable of self-regeneration? If after this war there is an interlude of complacent recovery in preparation for the next and more devastating visitation; if some imbecile return is made towards the *status quo ante*, with secularism rampant in education and Dr. Flexner perhaps "Dictator of Studies"; with the present smug and cynical substitute for democracy rampant and unashamed; with raw heresy masquerading under the name of "fraternal co-operation" and "glorious comprehensiveness"; with industrialism working again towards the final establishment of the Servile State; with a pseudo-evolutionary pseudo-philosophy salving the surface wounds of a vanishing conscience and feeding vanity with the pabulum of fatuous flattery; with public opinion and newspapers and automobiles and victrolas and airplanes and movies and "great white ways," and billionaires and war babies and pacifism and social-service crusades and world conferences on unfaith and disorder, —together with all the myriad other engaging manifestations of the era of enlightenment that succeeded the Christian Commonwealth of the Middle Ages—what are we to do?

Frankly, I think there is nothing but a raising of the cry "To your tents, O Israel!" and a retreat to the walled towns, that will be the new sanctuaries of those who are too proud to bend the knee to Baal: to voluntary "concentration camps," each of which would be a little *imperium in imperio*, an oasis of self-restraint in a desert of self-indulgence, where once more religion becomes something besides a social amenity and interpenetrates all life until again the bad division between Church and State is altogether lost. It is only in such communities that the human scale can be regained, and until this replaces the imperialism that now dominates all action and all thought, it is useless to talk about civilization as a thing which has any contemporary existence. Of course, each walled town would contain its twin kernel of life in the shape of a parish church and a monastery, the latter term covering houses both for men and women; therefore, even with this extension of the monastic idea, we shall need our cloisters of the olden type, and even more than otherwise. Of course, few of us have or will have the vocation to the Religious Life, and we shall need to preserve and restore the old and holy institution of the family. Therefore, if we are to be driven out, not into, but from, the wilderness man has made with his clever hands and cleverer brain, we must have our walled towns; but these can assemble better around the walls of some religious house than they can be created by fiat, while itself must be always the center of spiritual energy and the final refuge of those who have become weary of living even in the paradisaical peace of a walled town.

From every point of view the restoration and expansion of the consecrated Religious Life is the demand most clamorous today. Not that it may supersede the secular priesthood, but supplement and strengthen it; not that it may hold up an ideal of asceticism in place of that forever consecrated by the Holy Family of Nazareth, but by its own voluntary self-sacrifice, make the human family more secure in its place; not that it may destroy but that it may fulfill.

Five centuries ago, and a thousand, and fifteen hundred, and two thousand, the world in its periodical agony called aloud for aid, and men put all behind them and answered, in conformity with the will of our Lord and Savior Jesus Christ, Who first, for the saving of the world, voluntarily established for Himself and for those who would follow Him, the threefold vows of Poverty, Chastity and Obedience and added for full measure, Brotherhood and Work. Again the same call goes forth, and now, or later, the same answer must be made and will be made. If to any of you the call has ever come, "Sell that thou hast; take up thy cross and follow Me," he must make sure of two things: first, that the call is indeed of God; and second, that even at the price of life itself, it does not go unheeded.

SACRAMENTALISM AND THE FUTURE

SACRAMENTALISM IS THE DIVINE LAW of life and therefore it is the essential element, of the very *esse* of Catholic faith and Catholic philosophy, securing them in absolute isolation from all ethnic religions and the many inventions of man-made philosophies.

Here is the definition of a sacrament by the greatest expositor of sacramental philosophy, Hugh of St. Victor:

> The sacrament is the corporal or material element set out sensibly, representing from its similitude, signifying from its institution, and containing from its sanctification, some invisible and spiritual grace.

Then the greatest pure intellect, St. Thomas Aquinas, proceeds, in speaking of the Holy Sacrament of the Altar:

> All the other sacraments seem to be ordained to this one as to their end, for it is manifest that the sacrament of Order is ordained to the consecration of the Eucharist; and the sacrament of Baptism to the reception of the Eucharist; while a man is perfected by Confirmation so as not to fear to abstain from this sacrament. By Penance and Extreme Unction, man is prepared to receive the Body of Christ worthily, and Matrimony, at least in its signification, touches this sacrament; in so far as it signifies the union of Christ and the Church, of which union the Eucharist is a figure.

As, from the creation of the world, it has been a world of sacraments, so, from Pentecost, the Church has worked in and by the Seven Sacraments; it would be almost possible to say that the Church has existed *for* its sacraments, since these are the means ordained by God for particularizing the Redemption of Calvary in the person of every man, reconciling to Himself each who will and redeeming him from that slavery to matter in which he was bound through his inheritance. There is no Church without the sacraments. The apostolic ministry itself is ordered and perpetuated simply as the means of preserving the validity of the sacraments of Penance and of the Body and Blood of Christ, and as St. Thomas has said, even Penance is a means towards the Holy Sacrament of the Altar which is "the end and aim of all the sacraments."

I conceive that the time has come for us to take thought of the bearing of this on the question of our relationship to those, outside the communion of the Catholic Church, who deny the sacraments as such, accepting conditionally two of them only, and these simply as symbols or commemorative ceremonies. I conceive, also, that this scrutiny should extend to more intimate circles of affiliation. The famous Lambeth "Quadrilateral" is fatally weak in that it imposes the *fact* of the Apostolic Ministry without reference to its significance and its reason for being. What excuse has it except that it ensures the making of priests who can administer the sacrament of Penance, act as the agencies for the performing of the Divine miracle in Holy Mass; offer the very Body and Blood of Christ a Sacrifice before God, and to these ends ensure the unbroken continuance of a Catholic priesthood until the end of time.

Acceptance of the threefold ministry, and of the fact of Apostolic succession through the laying on of hands on the part of those who claim this tactual succession, if it did not carry with it a true acceptance of the Catholic doctrine of the nature, and efficacy, and mode of operation of the Seven Sacraments, would be but a still further extension of heresy closely approaching sacrilege. What we who are Catholics want and work for and pray for is unity in faith and belief even if there is some diversity in practice. We have come to the parting of the ways and can no longer follow a path that has led to substantial unity of practice with unlimited diversity in belief.

It is for this reason that we can take no further interest in an empty conformity; that the "glorious comprehensiveness" of last-century apologetic leaves us cold, and that at last we are coming to consider whether it is possible for any portion of the Church to remain longer half Protestant and half Catholic, mingled indifferently of those who accept and those who deny the Catholic doctrine of the sacraments. It is here that the line of demarcation exists; not between those who maintain the form of the threefold ministry and those who prefer the congregational polity; not between the adherents of a more or less historical liturgy and those who take unto themselves many inventions of curious and novel ritual; not between the Protestant Episcopalian and the Protestant Congregationalist whatever his sect and name, but between those who, on the one hand, accept the dogma and philosophy of sacramentalism, with the Seven Sacraments in their entirety, and the supreme sacrament of Holy Mass as the crown and consummation of all; and, on the other hand, those who reject the sacrament of Penance, turn the sacrament of Matrimony into a civil contract, ignore the sacraments of Confirmation and Unction, and recognize in the Sacrament of the Altar neither Sacrifice nor Real Presence, but only a symbolical commemoration of a *fait accompli*.

The division lies here and it is impossible. On the one hand lies Protestantism, on the other, Catholicism, and the two can never mix. On the one hand is that vast body of men in communion with the Apostolic See of Rome, the heterogeneous, if not heterodox, units of the fast crumbling Eastern Church, and—ourselves. On the other, all the one hundred and fifty-seven varieties of sects, together with a probable majority of the bishops, clergy and people of the Anglican and the Protestant Episcopal Churches. The line of cleavage lies here and not elsewhere, and nothing is gained by a denial of the fact.

It is not along this line, however, that I wish to speak; the place of the sacraments in Catholic Christianity, their essential nature, the supreme significance of the Sacrament of the Altar and its unique value devotionally, are all, for us, matters of common knowledge and need no argument. That, as St. Thomas says, "this sacrament is the end and consummation of all the sacraments," we know, but I do not think we sufficiently realize that behind lies a great, a complete system of philosophy, developed by, or revealed through, supreme exponents of Christian thought; a philosophy that underlies all the great Christian centuries, explaining their achievements, revealing their quality, making manifest their singularity in human life. A philosophy that is also a sufficient exposition of the universe, and that has been rejected through the last five-century epoch of modernism in favor of a materialistic system called Evolution, with the result we see before us in the progressive collapse, in horror, in ignominy and dishonor, of what we have called modern civilization. In an absolutely real sense it is possible to say that the rejection of sacramentalism and of the Catholic sacraments, in philosophy and religion, is the root cause of the war. And the corollary follows close upon; that is to say, it is only through the abandonment of evolutionary philosophy and a return, in spirit and in act, to an explicit and inclusive sacramentalism, that we can look for the energizing force that will enable us to build up a new world on the wide ruins of a great failure.

I would not minimize the great work we have to do in bringing *Ecclesia Anglicana* to recognize, accept and avow Holy Mass as the central, supreme and unique *Opus Dei* in her visible life and action; this cannot be too strongly emphasized, nor the equal duty in bringing again explicit recognition of the Mass as Sacrifice as well as Communion. The two things where effort should now be centered are, I believe, the establishing of Reservation as the standard practice in all churches, and the preaching of the Sacrifice of the Mass. Reservation by Episcopal tolerance, either as the result of good nature, indifference, or the working of "the principle of comprehensiveness," is unworthy and hardly to be tolerated except *faute de mieux*. I am not sure that the enforcing of the doctrine of the Eucharistic Sacrifice is not more important. Both work towards establishing the Real Presence of Christ in the Sacrament, and this is fundamental both from the standpoint of religion and of philosophy. St. Augustine has said: "Christ was sacrificed once in Himself, and yet He is sacrificed daily in the Sacrament," and St. Thomas, with that splendid lucidity that makes him "Doctor Angelicus,"

> This Sacrament is both a sacrifice and a sacrament; it has the nature of a sacrifice inasmuch as it is offered up, and it has the nature of a sacrament inasmuch as it is received. And therefore it has the effect of a sacrament in the recipient and the effect of a sacrifice in the offerer, or in them for whom it is offered.

Sacrament and Sacrifice, the two great realities the world had cast away during that era that is now coming to its unhonored end through such a cataclysm as has not happened since the fall of Rome. Through the Great Purgation of War and the universal testing of souls, the reality of sacrifice is coming back to a world that thought it could do without, but the reality of sacramentalism is still far from the minds of men. Still the world is enmeshed in the tangled web of a false philosophy; deep in the morass of dull materialism it struggles vainly, led to its betrayal by the *ignis fatuus* of an iridescent intellectualism. From this nemesis it must be saved if a new Dark Ages is to be avoided.

Let me quote again from Hugh of St. Victor, a great philosopher of the twelfth century, one who is little known but who is, I think, not only the perfect expositor of sacramentalism, but as great a philosopher under Christianity as Plato under paganism:

> There was a certain wisdom that seemed such to them that knew not the true wisdom. The world found it and began to be puffed up, thinking itself great in this. Confiding in its

> wisdom it became presumptuous and boasted it would attain the highest wisdom. And it made itself a ladder of the face of creation. ... Then those things which were seen were known, and there were other things which were not known; and through those which were manifest they expected to reach those that were hidden. And they stumbled and fell into the falsehoods of their own imagining. ... So God made foolish the wisdom of this world; and He pointed out another wisdom, which seemed foolishness and was not. For it preached Christ crucified, in order that truth might be sought in humility. But the world despised it, wishing to contemplate the works of God, which He had made a source of wonder, and it did not wish to venerate what He had set for imitation, neither did it look to its own disease, seeking medicine in piety; but presuming on a false health, it gave itself over with vain curiosity to the study of alien things.

I know not if there is anywhere a better description than this, of our own world of modernism that reached the summit of its ascending curve in the first decade of the present century. For four hundred years it had been progressively abandoning that sacramental idea that progressively had grown during the fifteen antecedent centuries under that constant and cumulative revelation that was promised and given to the Catholic Church. So in the end the world "stumbled and fell into the falsehoods of its own imagining," until "God made foolish the wisdom of this world" by permitting it to develop its logical conclusion in world war and irremediable ruin.

Any future of decency and righteousness must be based on a renunciation of "the wisdom of this world," which is materialism substantiated by the heresy of Evolution; so much of the Church as has adhered to sacramentalism, or recovered it after the episode of the Reformation, holds in its hands the keys to this future, and it will be largely, if not primarily, through the reinforcement of sacramentalism that the future may be assured. For us then, and for all Catholics, devotion to the Holy Sacrament of the Altar opens out into something far more than doctrine and worship; into the very philosophy and way of thought and mode of life that must condition society after the war.

We hear much of a new knowledge of Mediævalism and of a Mediæval revival. This is far more than a question of architectural style, more than an escape from contemporary imperialism into the free democracy of the Middle Ages, more than a restoration of the Mediæval industrial system. It is in effect a return to the religion and the philosophy of the Catholic ages which made possible Gothic art and the guild system and the social unit of human scale.

The world is ready for the great return. In four years war has shattered the whole brummagem[2] fabric of modernism. Industrial civilization, imperial nationalism, industry and finance, the intellectual criterion, automatic evolution, the omnipotence of education and environment, the possibility of earthly perfectibility for man, all have gone on the pyre of great burning, and only the penitential ashes remain. At the very moment when the whole world acclaimed triumphant modernism as victor over the slaughtered superstitions of the past, behold a great wonder; the casting down into the dust of the idols of brass and the naked showing of the clumsy feet of clay; yea, the world is ready, and more than ready, and the proclamation of old truth, long forgotten, will not fall on deaf ears.

---

[2] brummagem – cheap, showy, or counterfeit.

The whole world is sacramental, and the Seven of the Catholic Church are but the sign and symbol of the Universe. Let me quote again from Hugh of St. Victor.

> God set for man as a sign the sacraments of his salvation, in order that whosoever would apprehend them with right faith and firm hope might, though under the yoke, have some fellowship with freedom. ... For as there is body and soul in man, and in Scripture the letter and the sense, so in every sacrament there is a visible external which may be handled and the invisible within which is believed and taught.

And finally,

> The spirit was created for God's sake; the body for the spirit's sake, and the world for the body's sake, so that the spirit might be subject to God, the body to the spirit, and the world to the body.

Let us go on from this. Life as we know it, the life of this world, is the union of matter and spirit; and matter is not spirit, nor spirit matter, nor is one a mode of the other but they are two different creatures. Severance of matter and spirit, of body and soul, is death. That ancient heresy that matter is a figment of fancy, is revamped in these latter days for the wonder of delectation of disillusioned Protestants. It is a symbol of death. That modern heresy ingeniously devised for the infidel and the materialist, that spirit is only a mode of matter automatically evolved through biological processes, is also a symbol of death, if it is not death itself, or perhaps that awful and mysterious thing, "the sin against the Holy Ghost." Materialism on the one hand, transcendentalism on the other, when carried to their logical conclusion, are denial of the law of life. All the

Sacramentalism and the Future

world is but the redemption and transfiguring of matter through the interpenetration and the indwelling of spirit. We cannot know spirit except through the accidents of matter; we *may* not know matter except as it is irradiated by spirit. Says St. Thomas, "Human nature is such it has to be led by things corporeal and sensible to things spiritual and intangible," and that contemporary but unconscious follower of Aquinas, Henri Bergson, echoes him when he says, "The intellect is characterized by a natural inability to comprehend life" "for—we cannot too often repeat it—intelligence and instinct are turned in opposite directions, the former towards inert matter, the latter towards life. Intelligence by means of science, which is its work, will deliver up to us more and more completely the secret of physical operation; of life it brings us, and moreover only claims to bring us, a translation in terms of inertia." "Intuition" (a term chosen by Bergson to express what Cardinal Newman called "the spiritual power of assent," and not an altogether happy one) is alone able to afford us, through material mediumship, some adumbration[3] of the infinite. As this great modern philosopher has said with singular clarity,

> On our personality, on our liberty, on the place we occupy in the whole of nature, on our origin, and perhaps also on our destiny, it throws a light feeble and vacillating, but it none the less pierces the darkness of the night in which the intellect leaves us.

---

[3] adumbration - the act of giving the main facts and not the details about something.

Seers and prophets and the greatest of artists are indeed so closely in touch at times with pure spirit that they seem absolved from the necessities of ordinary men, receiving inspiration directly and without the intervention of material things, but this relationship is unconscious; they are channels, media, for the outpouring of Divine grace upon others than themselves. In a sense, then, they become the material element in the sacramental union of form and spirit. Infrequently appear men and women who in the state of ecstasy undeniably transcend human limitations, becoming for the moment united to God after a mystical fashion, but they are singular episodes well without the common limitations of men. For man as man the fact remains, that as he is compact of body and soul in a unity only dissolved by death, so for him there is no approach to the Absolute save through the mediumship of material things.

During the great Christian centuries of the Middle Ages this fact was universally understood and accepted. As Mr. Porter says in his recent book, "Beyond Architecture," "To the mediæval mind reality was but a symbol of unreality, matter but a reflection of the immaterial. Our earth became only a shadow of Heaven." Yes, but by symbolism matter became glorified; through its conjunction with spirit it became, as does the body of man, "the temple of the Holy Ghost." All the world of men and women, flowers and forests and kindly beasts, of changing seasons and mysterious elemental forces, became but an antitype of the Incarnation. Gothic art of every sort is as great as it is because of this. What were Reims once, and Soissons, before their martyrdom, but the transfiguring of stone and metal and wood; dead matter delved from the ground or hewn out of the forest, through the labor of man exalted into forms of absolute beauty that, because of this loving labor had been transformed into gifts worthy of giving back to God, and into a mysterious creation that in the words of Abbot Suger of St. Denis "was neither wholly of earth nor wholly of Heaven but a mystical blending of both," the very revelation to men of that which was beyond their grasp but not beyond their reach—the Beatific Vision of that absolute truth and absolute beauty that are God in His Heaven. It is no accident that Gothic art and sacramental philosophy and the exaltation of the Blessed Sacrament synchronized in these years of the Middle Ages, for they are varied manifestations of the same thing. It is no accident that the destruction of Gothic art and the acceptance of a materialistic philosophy and denial of the Incarnation have synchronized in these later years, for here also they are varied manifestations of the same thing.

Out of the Renaissance came the exaltation of the intellectual test and standard; out of Protestantism the denial of the reality of the sacraments and of sacramentalism. The revolutions of the eighteenth and nineteenth centuries enforced the new doctrines and spread them wide, and the industrial standards and methods of the last century have finally separated spirit from matter, cast it out into the limbo of exploded superstitions, and left only dead matter for our desire and acceptance—money, material advantage and force.

We look with disgust on the hedonistic revels of a dying Roman Imperialism; we turn in offense from the sordid corruption of the last years of the Dark Ages; we hold up to scorn and derision the gross licentiousness of Church and State in the Italy of the fifteenth century; but no one of these epochs, base as it is, records a lower fall than the manners and methods and morals of our own modernism when at last the severance had been accomplished and matter, unregenerated and unredeemed, had become Lord of the World, materialism its sacrosanct religion and its law of life.

The curse of this great apostasy lay overall the peoples that in predominant numbers had turned from the Catholic faith and had abandoned sacramental philosophy: on England, France, America, but chiefest of all on Germany, for there the process had begun and there it had reached its flower. Great in the eyes of men were the results achieved through this comprehensive apostasy; wealth without limit (though confined to the few); ingenious and amazing machines myriad in number and endlessly turning out more wealth; forces of nature harnessed and made the meek bond-slaves of men; intellectual capacity raised to new levels of competence and capable of justifying anything so long as it diverged sufficiently from ancient and once honorable standards. There was hardly a man in the spring of 1914 who would have denied that modernism had gloriously triumphed, and only a scattered few who doubted its eternity. Then came the epic catastrophe when in an hour the card-castle had crumbled about our ears. The efficiency of material imperialism swept back the inefficiency of an imperialized democracy, and so it has continued for four years. The boasted barriers against war or dissolution, erected one behind the other by finance, capitalism, a socialistic and organized proletariat, universal education, popular government, intellectual and spiritual emancipation, broke, toppled and dissolved, forming only vanishing and impotent ramparts against a triumphant Force released from all bondage to moral standards and spiritual laws.

What this has meant in national conduct on the part of the thus far triumphant power, in broken oaths and cynical lying, in sanctioned savagery, and beastliness that balks the most morbid imagination, I need not rehearse; it is part of the history of all time. We have been told that all this is the pathological phenomenon of a small clan of aristocratic rulers, and that the people themselves, the good, kind, Teutonic peasants and workmen, have no part therein, and must be coddled and humored so that they may be encouraged to cast off the alien and official incubus under which they groan in heavy bondage. We are told, but we do not believe; for during the last three years the revelations of popular character have been convincing, and we know that what we are fighting is a supreme autocracy, and more: it is a homogeneous group of peoples, and more: it is a motive and a force let loose in the world that reaches its tentacles out into all nations, and that must be destroyed, root and branch, if society is to survive, and such civilization as we have be not cut off by a new Dark Ages. What it is they mean, among the people themselves, is well set forth in a very recent German newspaper, where it is said (but not for foreign consumption):

> Fraud, embezzlement, peculation, deceit, immorality, lust, these unhappily are the characteristics of German domestic life of the present day. ... Our returning victorious warriors will be confronted with a terrible disillusionment,

and our children will look back on these years as a time of rampant barbarism, of unchecked criminality and utter absence of morals.

It is to this that the new philosophy and the non-religion of the post-mediæval epoch have led us; to the war that scourges the whole world, to a break-down of moral sense and of right standards that make such a war, its antecedents and its concomitants, a possibility. There are many streams of tendency threading the last four centuries that have brought this about, but we can no longer escape the conviction that it is through Protestantism, and especially through the Protestant denial of Catholic sacramentalism, that the strongest element finds its course.

This is inevitably the case. Through sacramentalism we see the sanctity of material things through their function as a vehicle of the spirit, as through the Incarnation we realize the sanctity of the human body that is its dwelling-place. There is nothing so mean that it may not take on glory through the power of the Holy Ghost, nothing that cannot serve as a channel of Divinity. Through sacramentalism we understand how all this finality we call the Absolute shines to us in symbol through all created things, so that only by their mediation may we lay hold on the mystical vision of God. Of all this the world, as such, has known nothing during the last century. Material things have been this and no more: dead lumps and clods, from the gold that has become the one desire of man, to the human body bought and sold and outraged as utterly as under black African slavery. The spiritual ideal that is the life of man, isolated from its material symbol, has ceased to manifest itself, and is therefore denied save as a by-product of biological processes. Even the pledged word, in itself a just symbol, even a "sacramental," has been degraded, and by intellectual processes untouched by the fire of spiritual perception, has been proved no more than the evanescent formula of a discredited epoch.

There are two alternatives, sacramentalism or materialism. In the great civilization of the Middle Ages, as this had its flowering and, in a sense, its sacramental expression in Reims Cathedral and Soissons, we may see what the one leads to; in the bestial destruction of Reims and Soissons—an act symbolical in itself—we see the significant issue of the other.

It would be an interesting task to take up one by one the seven sacraments of Catholicism and show how each has, beyond its own special power, a great significance for us at this black and portentous moment of the world, but this would mean not an essay but a volume. Each one of us can, however, make his own application of each sacramental verity—Baptism, Confirmation, Penance, Orders, Matrimony, Unction, and the Holy Eucharist. Poignantly and perfectly each expresses some vital truth, but of them all the last, the crown and consummation of all the sacraments and of all sacramentalism, has the most sublime significance. Think for a moment of this great mystery: the bread and wine of man's natural food transformed in a moment by the power of God and at the hands of His priest into the very Body and Blood of the Savior of the World, to be at the same time the spiritual food of man and the everlasting Sacrifice for the sins of the whole world. The faith that accepts this, even though it were universal, might not abolish sin or avert war, for man is man always and works after his own kind. It *would* prevent such a war as this, and such civilization as that out of which the war came, for out of sacramental faith and practice came honor, and truth and sacrifice.

And through the war they are coming back. The perfidy and dishonor of the universal enemy rebuild in the desperate crusaders of the new age, honor and steadfastness and righteous hate. Out of the broken oaths and the cynical duplicity and cold and Machiavellian craft of Teutonism comes a new sense of truth and justice for those who are aligned against it. Into a world of hedonism and self-indulgence and gross individualism the meaning of sacrifice returns in the thunders of unexampled war, and men, women, children, in the trenches, on the high seas, at home, in garden and workshop, find in the supreme sacrifice that is theirs to offer, the revelation of their own souls.

The world must be made over anew, in every big and every little thing; made over politically, socially, industrially, economically, educationally; but these reforms, drastic as they must be, well-intentioned as they may be, will prove only mechanistic and disappointing devices, doomed to follow in the long sequence of nineteenth-century nostrums and panaceas, unless the great fundamental reform is achieved in the spirit, impulse and vision of all the peoples of the world, the gaining back of the character-quality that can make success to come out of indifferent means, and assure to wise measures their full fruition: and this lies in the sphere of what we call religion and philosophy.

We may honestly strive to "make the world safe for democracy," to guarantee the self-determination of all peoples, to shake off from the throat of human society the

Sacramentalism and the Future 49

clutching fangs of imperial finance and Jewish internationalism, to destroy the five-century-long antithesis between capital and labor; we may strive even to restore in all things the unit of human scale—and our labors will go for little unless we can gain again the unity of the Catholic Faith and the dynamic force of sacramental, which is to say Christian, philosophy.

It is no exaggeration to say that the future of the world lies with those who unite in unflinching devotion to the Blessed Sacrament as verily and indeed the Communion of the true Body and Blood of Christ, and as well the eternal Sacrifice offered of God to God for the sins of the world, and equally for the quick and the dead. It is not only as a solemn and supreme method of devotion, it is not merely as the central, unique and essential act of worship no other device of clever ingenuity can supplant, that we work and pray for the restoration of Holy Mass to its Divinely ordained position; it is because it is the crux and the key to all that follows after, all that the world has abandoned to its grievous peril, and that must be restored if it is to continue. Reunion and unity center around this, and not in "World Conferences on Faith and Order," "Lambeth Quadrilaterals," or half-hearted schemes of compromise and approximation. "It is the Mass that matters," and this once won the rest is easy. And this is true of fields far beyond that of religion itself. I repeat, in the end the whole solution of the world-crisis lies here, and if by a miracle the whole world were to wake up and find itself Catholic in the sense in which it was Catholic from the year 975 to the year 1305, the future would hold for us clear assurance of the quick evanishment of our crowding problems and the swift achievement of a new era of righteous life. The miracle may be wrought, for miracles are now the only things on which we can rationally count with reasonable assurance; but we cannot act on that assumption, and therefore we are bound to labor consistently, if desperately, for bringing about the acceptable change by human means.

In so fighting it is, I think, necessary that we should now make an act of renunciation of our fear of words, for it is fear of words rather than of things that has left us weak and has paralyzed our efforts. The two words we have most feared are Mass and Sacrifice. Let us fear them no longer but use them frankly as avowing our honest faith. Let us use the word Mass because it is a symbol of that unity in the communion of the Apostolic See towards which we must look as the end of all projects of reunion. Because it means not only Communion but also Sacrifice, and therefore expresses the dual nature of this sacrament. Because it definitely excludes the interpretation of this sacrament, as no more than a symbolical commemoration, that is intolerable to the Catholic Faith. Let us frankly avow our adherence to the historic doctrine of the sacrificial nature of this sacrament, since without this there is no unmutilated Catholicity resting on the unbroken tradition and belief of the Catholic Church.

Both the great realities that are signified by these two words have their close application to the present world crisis. Holy Communion and Holy Sacrifice both lie closer to the sickness that has overwhelmed society than we ourselves are disposed to think, while for the great majority of men any hint of association is preposterous.

Sacramentalism and the Future 51

* * *

Materialism cannot remain the law of life, the lodestar of human endeavor; it cannot even exist in a world where all material things are seen to be only evanescent phenomena, where matter itself is recognized not only as the vehicle of the spirit and a means towards the achieving of spiritual vision, but also as impermanent world-stuff out of which, by essential transformation, something else is made, that thing for the achieving of which life, as we know life on this earth, exists. How thin, futile, inconsiderable, in the light of this vision, seem all those material ends and those material methods which for so many generations have been the base ideals of men. The sinister politics and oblique diplomacy, the delusive philosophies of evolutionists and pragmatists, the subterranean machinations of high finance and "big business," the gross opportunism of social systems, the ignoble warfare of industrial civilization, all show hollow and valueless in the light of spiritual revelation as this comes brokenly to us through the red tempest of war. Sooner or later, whether through victory or defeat (it is inevitable whatever the issue; the difference lies only in time), we shall confront the giant task of rebuilding a world. Let us see that our foundations are secure, for without them, deep-laid and firmly fixed, no superstructure of human ingenuity will stand for a generation.

Greater than the deliberations of Peace Conferences with their paper treaties, greater than new constitutions and novel frontiers, greater than political and industrial and social devices sprung from the fertile brains of ingenious artificers, will be the determinations of religion and philosophy. Thus far, since the battle cry of Armageddon sounded on those last days of July 1914, neither has played a prominent or even a creditable part. From the Cardinal of Malines to the priest soldiers in the trenches and the chaplains of many faiths, there are endless instances of individual nobility and heroism, and the list of martyrs and confessors increases daily. For the Church itself, whether Roman, Anglican, or Eastern, very little can be said; and less is said. The ominous fact is that it was and is a negligible factor. The same is true of the Protestant sects in their corporate capacity, whether they are the obedient sycophants of German autocracy or the free associations of England and America. Organized religion, Catholic and Protestant, has not only failed to meet the crisis in any measurable degree, or to adapt itself to the enormous agony of uncounted millions, it has sunk out of sight so far as world-forces are concerned, and its word, if uttered, would now go unheard. In the greatest cataclysm since the fall of Rome the Church has ceased to function as an operative, public force.

So with philosophy. In Germany the men once so inordinately famous (I know not why) just before the war, the Euckens and their kind, have become the apologists of dishonor. The greatest figure in France, Bergson, is silent before a crisis he cannot meet, and among English-speaking people we have only a Father Figgis or a Chesterton to fight through the blind chaos in the desperate endeavor to find some signs of a philosophy of life that may clear the way for that which is to come. Not alone were we unprepared in a political, industrial, economic and military sense to meet the assault of a conscienceless and efficient enemy, our unpreparedness extended equally to the categories of philosophy and religion, and we suffer, and may in the end fail, quite as much on account of one as of the other.

Thus far we have failed, but we can always look to the future, and it is never too late for amendment, even for the winning of salvation. I cannot presume to speak for the Church of Rome, whose defects and delinquencies are other than our own. I do not propose to speak for Protestantism, which must act in accordance with its own principles, which are so different from those of Catholicism that no common ground appears. For ourselves, members of the Anglican Church, I see the need of new and radically different action along many lines; but none is more vital, more immediate in its necessity, more closely connected with the vast problem of the World after the War, than those I postulated at the beginning of this essay: sacramentalism as the basic philosophical system of the Church; the Seven Sacraments as its fundamental mode of operation; Holy Mass as the central fact of its worship and its Divine strength, and the reality and efficacy of the Eucharist Sacrifice.

THE PHILOSOPHICAL NECESSITY

"THEY ARE CALLED WISE who put things in their right order and control them well." So begins the first sentence of the "Summa Contra Gentiles" of St. Thomas Aquinas. The implied condemnation of those who establish false standards of comparative value and ill control those erroneously fixed, holds today as it held in the year 1262, even though now they may be a preponderant multitude where then they were a minor if conspicuous faction.

"To put things in their right order and control them well"; is not this the essence of wisdom and the secret of righteous life? To weigh and assort all things, estimating the value of each in relation to all others and to eternal truth; to exalt and pursue the things that are great and admirable and everlasting; to cast down and reject those things that are insignificant and transitory and without value. This is the substance of wisdom, as it is the object of each man's living; that he may control them well, both the great things and the small, not with fumbling hands and by unstable minds swayed by every wind of doctrine aroused by Roger Bacon's *vulgi sensus imperiti*, but with the firm grasp of mastership directed by an intrepid and reasonable mind.

This is that Wisdom that is the eternal goal of intellectual man, and *Philosophia* the way of that everlasting pilgrimage. "Philosophy," says the great Cardinal of

Malines, "is the science of the totality of things. The particular sciences are directed to groups of objects more or less restricted; philosophy, the general science, regards the sum-total of reality." So it appears that philosophy alone enables us to "put things in their right order" when the accidents and illusions of life, and the narrow outlook of the single sciences, have confused all relations; and without a right philosophy we are as those of whom Hugh of St. Victor speaks who "stumbled and fell into the falsehoods of their own imaginings."

But the boon of a right philosophy is not the wages of a delving intellectuality nor is it the laurel crown of profound erudition. They that are thus furnished may attain the highest good, as Aristotle and St. Thomas Aquinas, but achievement is granted also to the humble and the unlearned; the shepherd on the hills, the poet in bitter exile, the monk in his forgotten cloister. There is much truth in the words of Friar Bacon: "All the wisdom of philosophy is created by God and given to the philosophers, and it is Himself that illuminates the minds of men in all wisdom." This is necessarily so; from Aristotle to the modern Aquinas, Henri Bergson, every philosopher who can justly claim the title has based his system on the primary assumption that man, of his own motion, cannot remotely touch the "thing-in-itself," the *noumenon*, the Absolute, but is able to deal only with the phenomenon or, as Aristotle calls it, the "phantasm." "In the present state of life, in which the soul is united to a passible body," says St. Thomas, "it is impossible for our intellect to understand anything actually, except by turning to the phantasm"; and Bergson says the same when he states as an axiom that "the mind of man by its very nature is incapable of apprehending reality." Philo, the Platonist Jew, put it succinctly when he wrote, "The trammels of the body prevent men from knowing God in Himself; He is known only in the Divine forces in which He manifests Himself."

Yet if we would live we must be able "to put things in their right order," and to know God in the sense of personal approach if not of comprehension. It is here that the love of God shows itself in that He does again and again reveal enough of the everlasting wisdom and of Himself to enable men to assure themselves that He is, and, if they will, to turn their footsteps in the right way.

Through the Incarnation came not only the Redemption but also the Enlightenment, and thereafter the order of the Universe and the significance of life were as clear as they may ever be without a further explicit revelation; but "God has never left Himself without a witness," and so five centuries before the Incarnation, and since then amongst those who knew not Christ, much has been revealed, so that great philosophers have appeared and have spoken "with the tongues of men and angels," and the things that we may use for our soul's health today, when in our own time, with all our erudition and our scientific attainment and our stored-up knowledge of centuries, the Divine revelation has not come, and we have not only forgotten or rejected the philosophy of the inspired men of the past, but as well have taken to ourselves those that spoke without God, makers of false philosophies, and so have "fallen into the falsehoods of our own imaginings."

In this fact lies not only the reason why the world in spite of its material glory dipped lower and lower towards the point of disaster achieved in July A.D. 1914, but the explanation of the notorious inability of both organized religion and formal philosophy to meet the challenge of a world in dissolution during four years of war, and finally the lack of a great, constructive, dynamic leading on, at this moment when the destinies of man are being determined for a period of five centuries. There is today no operative philosophy of life; we are trifling with the shreds and shards of the materialistic and mechanical substitutes of the eighteenth and nineteenth centuries, from Descartes to Herbert Spencer, from Hobbes and Kant to Nietzsche and William James, and in them there is neither health nor safety, nor the clear conviction, the lucid and logical organism, the invigorating and passionate force of the Athenians, the Fathers of the Church, the Neo-Platonists or the mighty masters of Mediævalism.

The Reformation destroyed more for us of the North and the West than the fabric of the Catholic Church and the substance of the Catholic Faith. The nexus between theology and philosophy is so close that what affects one affects the other. "*Intellige ut credas; crede ut intelligas*," says St. Augustine. It is not so much that theology begins where philosophy leaves off, and *vice versa*, as it is that both pursue an actually parallel course in time, and side by side; if one falls the other stumbles, and unless quick recovery is effected both are involved in a common ruin. I do not know which stumbled first at that critical moment when Mediævalism yielded to the Renaissance. Machiavelli wrote "Il Principe" in 1513, Luther posted his Theses in 1517, and the protagonist of the assault on Catholic philosophy and ethics would thus appear to have an advantage of some four years over the protagonist of the assault on Catholic theology and religion. On the other hand, while the new paganism in philosophy does not antedate the fall of Constantinople in 1453, the particular form of heresy that was to rend the unity of the Church for the latest time and plunge entire nations in centuries of heresy and schism, had shown itself sporadically more than a hundred years before. The question is of no importance; the first breakdown of Catholic theology and Catholic philosophy practically synchronized during the period known as the Reformation, and wherever the Faith was abandoned the philosophy went with it.

Our own epoch, modernism (as one should say Mediævalism, or the Dark Ages or Roman Imperialism), the five hundred years extending from the formal end of the Middle Ages in 1453, to 1953—or whatever may be the year when the next epoch is determined for good or ill, —is that period during which the peoples that rejected both Catholic theology and Catholic philosophy, or tolerated both with a thin formalism that voided them of all power, have directed the development of society and determined the lives of its peoples up to and including its climacteric in the Great War. Whether they were worth having at the price, this new religion and this new philosophy—or rather *these*, for the diversity is extreme—does not concern me at this present. The point I wish to make is that as those two things, each unique in its sphere, made possible the five centuries of Mediæval civilization which formed the most successful exposition of Christianity that has thus far been achieved, and that as their obliteration is responsible for the civilization (however we may estimate it) that has now succeeded in destroying itself after a remarkable dominion of other five centuries, so the future, the foundations of which we have now to lay, can only approach in dignity, nobility and achievement the Christian centuries of the Middle Ages if we are willing and able to forsake modernist religion and modernist philosophy and return explicitly to the religion and the philosophy of that incomparable olden time. In a word, a sane and wholesome and just and righteous future can be built only on the corner-stones of Catholic religion and sacramental philosophy.

For once it is not necessary to argue over the matter of religion; the logic of events has dealt with that and fixed its own determinations. The question of philosophy is in a different category. We have so long been accustomed to live without a philosophy and to take refuge in archæology and "the appeal to history" and the flimsy scaffoldings of Teutonism or Evolutionism or Pragmatism, we neither feel the need of this strong defense, this vast directing energy, nor take kindly to it when it is offered. Yet there can be no right and enduring religion without a right philosophy, as there can be no right and enduring philosophy without a right religion. "Philosophy is the science of the totality of things." "They are called wise [that is to say, philosophers] who put things in their right order and control them well." "Philosophy regards the sum-total of reality." The moment has come for us to see things as a whole, to establish a new system of comparative values, to confront not fictions but realities. "The integrity of our nature is repaired by wisdom," wrote St. Vincent of Beauvais. Reparation lies before us, —of our nature, of society and of the world, — and to that end we must turn to philosophy, that as ever it may fortify the impulse of religion and by religion be irradiated by the grace of God.

What then is this philosophy of the Middle Ages that is in itself as definitive as the Catholic Faith? It is no ethnic or passing intellectual by-product; it is the synthesis of antecedent philosophies, Neo-Platonic, Jewish, Arabian, Byzantine, Patristic, Peripatetic, Socratic, purged of their alien elements, gathered into an organic unity, and vitalized by the Catholic religion. Its greatest exponents are St. Thomas Aquinas, Duns Scotus and Hugh of St. Victor. It was this philosophy that, consciously or unconsciously, formed the substance of the wisdom of the peoples of the Middle Ages, conditioning all their acts and all their intellectual processes. As, with the Catholic religion, it was the energizing force in life, making possible the only consistent Christian civilization thus far achieved, so was it the full rounding out of a great culture that re-created all the arts for its own expression, invented new ones, and raised them all to a level of unexampled achievement. Its abandonment synchronized, if it did not compass, the fall of Christian civilization and the entrance of the New Paganism which has now, in its turn, met its nemesis in its own suicidal aggrandizement.

In trying to express in brief and suggestive form this philosophy of sacramentalism, I have not confined myself to any one system, neither to the Dominican, the Franciscan nor the Augustinian synthesis; I have tried to establish a working theory by a molding together of all three (since for all practical purposes this is what historically happened) and I have not disdained a return, on occasion, to the Neo-Platonists, particularly Plotinus, and to the Greek and

Jewish philosophers themselves, from whom all their successors have learned much and at whose feet they have sat as respectful scholars. Daring much in this process, I have doubtless fallen into philosophical error, and perhaps have even offended against dogmatic truth, but I profess here and now that I submit all I say to Catholic Authority, and that I desire to teach nothing contrary to the Catholic Faith.

The world as we know it, man, life itself as it works through all creation, is the union of matter and spirit; and matter is not spirit, nor spirit matter, nor is one a mode of the other, but they are two different creatures. Apart from this union of matter and spirit there is no life in the sense in which we know it, and severance is death. "The body," says St. Thomas, "is not of the essence of the soul; but the soul by the nature of its essence can be united to the body, so that, properly speaking, the soul alone is not the species, but the composite," and Duns Scotus makes clear the nature and origin of this common "essence" when he says there is "on the one hand God as Infinite Actuality, on the other spiritual and corporal substances possessing a homogeneous common element." That is to say, both matter and spirit are the result of the Divine creative act and though separate and opposed find their common point of departure in the Divine Actuality.

The created world is the concrete manifestation of matter through which, for its own transformation and redemption, spirit is active in a constant process of interpenetration, whereby matter itself is being eternally redeemed. What then is matter, and what is spirit? In the theory of Plotinus, the process of emanation from a Supreme Principle, the one source of all existing things, explains the physical and metaphysical worlds. According as the principle gives out its energy, it exhausts itself, its determinations follow a descending scale, becoming less and less perfect. Every generative process implies a decadence or inferiority in the generated product. And in the series of Divine generations there must be a final stage, at which the primal energy, weakened by successive emissions, is no longer capable of producing anything real. A limit is necessarily reached beneath which there cannot be anything less perfect; this limit is *matter*. Matter is merely the space which conditions all corporate existence; it is a pure possibility of being, mere nothingness, and is identified with primitive evil.

In the sense he clearly intends, Plotinus' theory of "emanation" is of course superseded by the Christian doctrine of creation, but it was an illuminating approximation to final truth. Similarly, God cannot exhaust Himself, but there is manifestly a great discrepancy in point of perfection between the angels at one end of the scale, and simple matter, before form is given it, at the other, while in between are the many categories of creation. Neither is matter "mere nothingness," for it is a created thing, therefore it exists, even without form. I do not quote Plotinus as authoritative, but rather as one who through "natural" revelation has approached closely to the truth of Divine revelation.

Subjected to certain necessary changes in terminology I cannot see why this definition of matter does not coincide with Duns Scotus' *Materia primo prima*, which is thus described by the great Franciscan.

Materia primo prima is the indeterminate element of contingent things. This does not exist in Nature, but it has reality in so far as it constitutes the term of God's creative activity. By its union with a substantial form it becomes endowed with the attributes of quantity and becomes *secundo prima*. Subject to the substantial changes of Nature it is matter as we perceive it.[4]

It is this *materia primo prima*, "the term of God's creative activity," that is eternally subjected to the regenerative process of spiritual interpenetration, and the result is organic life.

Is this matter "primitive evil" in the sense in which Plotinus uses it? No, for *omne ens est bonum* and because "God made all things good from the beginning." On the other hand, matter is in itself dead, inert, constantly exerting on spirit a gravitational pull that must be overcome. In a real sense, therefore, its inertness does manifest itself as "evil" since its resistance to spirit is actual and must be overcome.

What is "spirit" as the term is used here? The creative Power of the Logos, in the sense in which St. John interprets and corrects the early, partial and erroneous theory of the Stoics and of Philo. God the Son, the Eternal Word of the Father, "the brightness of His glory and the figure of His substance." "God of God, Light of Light, very God of very God, begotten not made, being of one substance with the Father, by whom all things were made." Pure wisdom, pure intellect, pure will, unconditioned by matter, but creating life out of the operation of His Spirit on and through matter,

---

[4] Plotinus calls matter "the limit" of Divine generation because it marks the exhaustion of creative activity. Scotus calls it "the term" because beyond it God did not will to extend this creative activity.

and in the fullness of time becoming Incarnate for the purpose of the final redemption of man.

Now since man is so compact of matter and of spirit, it must follow that he cannot lay hold of that pure spirit, that Absolute that lies beyond and above all material conditioning, except through the medium of matter, through its figures, its symbolism, its "phantasms." Says St. Thomas, "From material things we can rise to some kind of knowledge of immaterial things, but not to the perfect knowledge thereof." The way of life, therefore, is the increasing endeavor of man to approach the Absolute through the leading of the Holy Spirit, so running parallel to that slow perfecting of matter which is being effected by the same operation. So matter takes on a certain sanctity, not only as something in process of perfection, but as the vehicle of spirit and its tabernacle, since in matter spirit is for us in a sense incarnate.

From this process follows of necessity the whole sacramental system of the Catholic Church, as this is set over against both the Protestant theory and that of modernist symbolism. To the Protestant as to the Jew the material thing is (though only in theory) incorrigibly base, to be despised and treated with contempt, while the spiritual thing, the soul, may and does unite itself to, and perfectly achieve union with ultimate spirit directly, without the intervention of the material vehicle, and in proportion to its isolation from matter. The Protestant rejects even the value of the symbol; the modern symbolist, or ritualist if you like the word better, sees the symbol and values it, but he does not recognize the reality behind the symbol, contenting himself with what is no more than a form of poetry or other art, and he no more achieves either a right philosophy, the real religion, or that mystical union with God that is his aim, than does the Protestant or the scientific rationalist. I speak of generalities; there are anomalous personalities that, for His own ends, God gives that Beatific Vision that "o'erleaps the bounds" of matter, whereby the law of life is for them superseded and the material nexus is abrogated. These are the prophets, seers, mystics, —the greatest artists perhaps as well, —but they are not properly of this world as we know it; for the vast majority of men the way of matter is the road proscribed.

How fatal is this pseudo-philosophy that would cleave life in halves by isolating matter on one side and spirit on the other, is shown by the experience of those who accepted it. Rejecting the Sacraments as Divine channels of grace ordered and established for the transfusion through material agencies of the power of God the Holy Ghost, and denying even the value of their symbolism; denouncing the priesthood as a man-made obstacle between the created and the Creator; scorning the body and condemning all material things as hateful and as stumbling-blocks; they nevertheless became the proponents of aggressive materialism; organizers of industrialism, creators of "big business" and "high finance," exploiters of labor and of markets, prophets of a civilization of greed, covetousness and profiteering. It is the Protestant nations and their *enclaves* of Jews that built up that materialistic civilization that in its bloated triumph finds its own nemesis in the war of the last five years and the events that are to follow in the five next years that are to come. The material thing is deadly only when it is cut off from the spiritual thing; united, matter ennobled as an agent, spirit familiarized through its homely housing, we have that just balance which has issue in a culture and a civilization such as that of the Middle Ages.

Sacramentalism, in theology, in discipline and in philosophy, is the essential system of Christianity, and it follows inevitably from the fundamental doctrines of the Incarnation and the Redemption. Those portions of the Church of Christ that adhere to it in its three manifestations will endure, the others will wither away. Furthermore, no compromise is possible any more than compromise is possible with truth. As the time came when America could no longer exist half slave and half free, so the time has now come (and the warning has been explicit) when the Church can no longer exist under the same conditions.

As the rejection of the Seven Sacraments deprived northern Europe of that stream of spiritual energy, forever, and by the covenant of God, coursing through the several material channels of operation, leaving man bereft of his surest reinforcement against the eternal gravitational pull of matter; as the abandonment of Catholic order and discipline unloosed the floods of intellectual insolence and vulgarian presumptuousness, cleaving Christianity in halves and reducing the moiety[5] thereof into a howling chaos of ill-conditioned heresies, so the forsaking of sacramental philosophy left life meaningless except as a sort of neo-Manicheism as exploited by Calvin and the Puritans, and as an everlasting warfare, the prize of which was material gain through power or money, as was demonstrated (though not

---

[5] moiety- each of two parts into which a thing is or can be divided.

always avowed) by the creators and beneficiaries of industrial civilization. The nineteenth century philosophy of Evolution with its dogmas of the struggle for life, and the survival of the fittest, was the effort of sincere men to cast a veil of respectability over a thing in itself ignominious and unchristian, and the results of its acceptance have recently been demonstrated to admiration.

Dualism is the destroyer of righteousness, and the Catholic philosophy of sacramentalism is the antithesis of dualism. The sanctity of matter as the potential of spirit and its dwelling-place on earth; the humanizing of spirit through its condescension to man through the making of his body and all created things its earthly tabernacle, give, when carried out into logical development, a meaning to life and a glory to the world and an elucidation of otherwise unsolvable mysteries, and an impulse towards noble living, neither Protestantism nor even Christian Science can afford. It is a real philosophy of life, a standard of values, a criterion of all possible postulates, and as its loss meant the world's death, so its recovery may mean its resurrection.

In harmony with this consummate philosophy, and as its inevitable corollary, came the whole sacramental system of the Church, whereby every material thing was recognized as possessing in varying degree sacramental potentiality, while seven great Sacraments were instituted to be, each after its own fashion, a special channel for the influx of the power of God the Holy Ghost. Each was a symbol, a "phantasm," to use the word of Aristotle, just as so many other created things were, or could become, symbols, but beyond this they were realities, veritable *media* for the veritable communication of veritable Divine grace. Voided of power, reduced to the status of mere symbols, they become nothing; only the sentimental stimuli of personal emotion. There is no better definition of a Sacrament than that of Hugh of St. Victor:

> The Sacrament is the corporeal or material element set out sensibly, representing from its similitude, signifying from its institution, and containing from its sanctification, some invisible and spiritual grace.

This is the unvarying and unvariable doctrine of the Catholic Church; and the reason for its existence as a living and functioning organism, and the very methods of its operation, follow from this supreme institution of the Sacraments. The whole sacramental system is in a sense an extension of the Redemption, and one Sacrament, the Eucharist, also in a sense an extension of the Incarnation, just as it is also a daily, even hourly, extension *in time* of the Sacrifice of Calvary. The Church considered as simply the fellowship of the faithful is not an organism, it is an emotion. The Catholic Church is more than this; it is a living organism, and as such it is subject to the definite, explicit and unchanging laws of its organic system. What happens to the individual when he ceases to be a justly co-ordinated organism is demonstrated in countless insane asylums. What happens to a State under similar conditions is accomplished by Russia and is in process of evolution in Germany, if not throughout modern society. Indeed, Protestantism itself is sufficient evidence of the disastrous results that follow from such an abnormal course.

The Incarnation and the Redemption are not accomplished facts, completed nineteen centuries ago, they are processes that still continue, and their term is fixed only by the total regeneration and perfecting of matter, and the Seven Sacraments are the chiefest among an infinity of sacramental processes which are the agencies of this eternal transfiguration.

Christ not only became Incarnate to accomplish the Redemption of men as yet unborn, for endless ages, through the completed Sacrifice of Calvary, but also to initiate a new method whereby the results were to be more perfectly attained; that is to say, the Church, working through the specific sacramental agencies He had ordained or was later to ordain through His direction of the Church He had brought into being at Pentecost. He did not come to ordain a revolutionary code of ethics or even to offer in His own Person a new Model for human following. He was neither a newer Socrates nor an older Buddha, but God Himself, revealing the whole system of life and the reason for the world, and, through the New Covenant of the Catholic Sacraments and the One, Indivisible Catholic Church preserved from error in its official determinations in faith and morals, by virtue of His Presence therein until the consummation of the world, to fix this method of salvation in terms and under conditions identical with the process of life itself, and in forms fitted to the comprehension of, and freely available for, every man that is born of woman.

He did not come to establish in material form a Kingdom of Heaven on earth or to provide for its ultimate coming. He indeed established a Spiritual Kingdom, His Church, "in the world, not of it," but this is a very different matter—as the centuries have proved. His Kingdom is not of this world, nor will it be established here. The folly and the conceit of nineteenth century evolutionists have received their quietus during the last few years. There has been no *absolute* advance in human development since the Incarnation, nor yet during the space of recorded history. Nations rise and fall, epochs wax and wane, civilizations grow out of savagery, crest, and sink back into savagery again. Redemption is for the individual, not for the race nor yet for society as a whole, nor even for matter itself *except* as this becomes definite and concrete in the individual; and there, and only there, and under that form, it is sure, however long may be the period of its accomplishment. "Time is the ratio of the resistance of matter to the interpenetration of Spirit" and by this resistance is the duration of time determined. When it shall have been wholly overcome then "time shall be no more." God the Holy Ghost, proceeding from the Father and the Son, and by the channel of each individual soul, operates directly on the matter which in human form is the object of redemption, and the Sacraments are not only the Divinely ordained agencies of this operation but the perfect symbols of life itself.

See therefore how perfect is the correspondence between the Sacraments and the method of life where they are the agents and which they symbolically set forth. There is in each case the material form and the spiritual substance or energy. As Hugh of St. Victor says, each represents from its similitude, signifies from its institution, and contains from its sanctification some invisible and spiritual grace. Water, chrism, oil, the spoken word, the touch of the hands, the sign of the cross, and finally and supremely the bread and wine of Holy Mass, each a material thing but each representing, signifying and containing some gift of the Holy Spirit, real, absolute and potent. So matter and spirit are linked together in every operation of Holy Church from the cradle to the grave, and man has ever before him the eternal revelation of this linked union of matter and spirit in his life, the eternal teaching of the honor of the material thing through its agency and through its existence as the subject for redemption, while through the material association and the Divine condescension to his earthly and fallible estate (limited by the association with matter to only inadequate presentation) he makes the spirit of God his own, to dwell therewith after the fashion of man.

As I have said elsewhere,

> Man approaches, and must always approach, spiritual things not only through material forms but by means of material agencies. The highest and most beautiful things, those where the spirit seems to achieve its loftiest reaches, are frequently associated with the grossest and most unspiritual material forms, yet the very splendor of the spiritual verity redeems and glorifies the material agency, while on the other hand the homeliness and even animal quality of the material thing brings to man, with a poignancy and an appeal that are incalculable, the spiritual thing that in its absolute essence would be so far beyond his ken[6] and his experience and his powers of assimilation that it would be inoperative.

This is the true Humanism, not the fictitious and hollow thing that was the offspring of Neo-Paganism and took to itself a title to which it had no claim. Held consciously or tacitly by the men of the Middle Ages from the immortal

---

[6] ken - knowledge, understanding, or cognizance.

philosopher to the immortal but nameless craftsman, it was the force that built up the noble social structure of the time and poised man himself in a sure equilibrium. Already it had of necessity developed the whole scheme of religious ceremonial and given art a new content and direction through its new service. By analogy and association all material things that could be so used were employed as figures and symbols, as well as agencies, through the Sacraments, and after a fashion that struck home to the soul through the organs of sense. Music, vestments, poetry and dramatic action, incense, candles, flowers, all were linked with the great arts of architecture, painting and sculpture, and all became not only ministers to the emotional faculties but direct appeals to the intellect through their function as poignant symbols. So art received its soul, and was almost a living thing until matter and spirit were again divorced in the death that severed them during the Reformation, and thereafter religion entered upon a period of slow desiccation and sterilization wherever the symbol was cast away with the Sacraments and the sacramental philosophy that had made it live. Indifference or hostility to the pregnant and evocative and supremely beautiful ceremonial of the Catholic Faith is less ignorance of the meaning and function of art and an inherited hatred of its quality and its power, than they are the natural reactions of the conscious and determined rejection of the essential philosophy of the Catholic Church, which is sacramentalism.

With the first perfecting of this philosophy during the twelfth and thirteenth centuries along the three parallel lines of Hugh of St. Victor, Duns Scotus and St. Thomas Aquinas, came concurrently the brief but glorious flowering of Christian civilization from 1050 to 1300. It was then that not only philosophy, but theology, education, literature and all the old regenerated arts, and many new arts as well, achieved a sort of grand climacteric. It was during the same period that human society, political, industrial and economic, accomplished its highest perfection under Christianity, and the force widespread throughout the social organism concentrated itself in such focal points of dazzling light as St. Louis, St. Thomas and Dante, the Arthurian legend, the perfected Gregorian music and Reims Cathedral.

The whole sacramental system of philosophy was of an almost sublime perfection and simplicity, and the Catholic Sacraments were both its goal and its types. If they had been of the same value and identical in nature they would have failed of perfect exposition, in the sense in which they were types or symbols. They were not this, for while six of the explicit seven were sufficiently of one mode, there was one where the conditions that held elsewhere were transcended and where, in addition to the two functions it was instituted to perform, it gave through its similitude the clear revelation of the most significant and pregnant fact in the vast mystery of life. I mean of course the Holy Eucharist.

I desire to approach this consideration with the most complete abasement and profound reverence. I am not unmindful of the wise saying of St. Thomas a Kempis "'Twere well not to inquire too curiously into the nature of this Sacrament," but it is impossible to complete the consideration of what is the essential philosophy of Christianity unless this point is made clear. The designation, the nomenclature, dates back perhaps no farther than Hildebert of Tours in the eleventh century; the *fact* is attested as a theological and philosophical proposition by Paschasius Radbertus two centuries earlier, that is to say, in the time of Charlemagne. I refer to the dogma of Transubstantiation as expressing the manner whereby the Real Presence of God Incarnate is accomplished in the Holy Eucharist.

Now, in the first place, I wish to protest against two statements that are frequently made by those who are inimically disposed towards this doctrine. First, that it is only a quibbling over definitions that do not effect the fact; second, that defense of Transubstantiation is an affected and antiquarian attempt to restore a detail of an outworn scholasticism. I maintain that neither is true, but that, on the contrary, Transubstantiation meets a philosophical necessity inherent in the system of sacramentalism which is afforded by no other assumption whatever. There are four possible theories: *1st*, the Zwinglian, which as has been said, actually amounts to the "real absence" and may be disregarded, since it is contradicted by Christ Himself, has no place in historic Christianity back to the Apostolic Fathers, and is rejected by *Ecclesia Anglicana* and even by the Lutheran and Westminster Confessions; *2nd*, the Lutheran, that is to say, consubstantiation; *3rd*, the theory of Osiander, sometimes called "impanation," where Christ is really present through an hypostatic union; these last two covering, I suppose, the beliefs of the great majority of Anglicans; and there is finally the Catholic doctrine of Transubstantiation.

I am speaking now wholly from a philosophical standpoint. It is perhaps true that the doctrines of Osiander and Luther, as these are interpreted by Anglicans, are sufficient

The Philosophical Necessity 75

from a theological and a devotional standpoint. If life is what it is held to be by the philosophy of the Catholic Church, then the Catholic theory (or dogma, as it has been since the Council of Trent) is the only one which completes, by its symbolism and its assertion of fact, the sacramental showing forth, through great symbols, of the nature of life.

Under all other interpretation of this great Mystery, which is the crown of all the Sacraments, it does not differ from them except in degree; as in the case of the water of Baptism, the material agent remains unchanged, —it is matter still, precisely as before the words and acts of Consecration. The wafer is still unleavened bread, the wine and water have not changed in character; they have simply become the vehicle whereby God gives Himself to man. At the most the substance, bread, and the Substance, the Body of Christ, exist together after a mystical manner, *i.e.* through consubstantiation.

This doctrine of the Real Presence leaves the elements essentially unchanged, not only in their substance but in their accidents; but by spiritual interpenetration they become for the communicant, the offerer of the Holy Sacrifice, and those for whom it is offered, the Body and Blood of Christ. On the other hand the Catholic doctrine is that by the act of Consecration the very substance of the bread and wine are transformed into an altogether different Substance, the very Body and Blood of Christ, only the accidents of form, color, ponderability, etc., remaining.

It would be presumptuous for me to compare or contrast these two views of the Blessed Sacrament from a religious standpoint. Speaking philosophically, the doctrine of Transubstantiation certainly reveals and substantiates a great principle that may be the very secret of life itself and the reason for the existence of the world, while its abandonment by Protestants, not to mention infidels and agnostics, lies close at the root of that materialism that has reached its logical climax in the present world-wide catastrophe.

If matter is forever matter, inert, unchangeable, indestructible, then it is hard to escape the sense of dualism in the universe: matter and spirit uniting in man as body and soul, in the sacraments as the vehicle and the essence, but temporally and temporarily; doomed always to ultimate severance either by death or by the completion of each sacramental process. Suppose, on the other hand, the object of the universe and of time is the constant redemption and transformation of matter, through its interpenetration by spirit through the power of God the Holy Ghost. Suppose that the miracle of Transubstantiation is but the type and showing forth of the incessant process of life whereby, every instant, matter itself is being changed and glorified, and transferred from the plane of matter—the earth-plane—to the plane of spirit—the heavenly plane. Is not this the meaning of St. Paul's "There is an earthly body and there is a spiritual body; we are sown in corruption, we are raised in incorruptibility."

If this is so, if the Incarnation and Redemption are types and symbols of the Divine process forever proceeding here on earth, then while the other Sacraments are in themselves not only agencies of grace, but manifestations of that process whereby in all things matter is used as the vehicle of the spirit, the Mass, transcending them all, is not only Communion, not only a Sacrifice for the quick and the dead acceptable before God, but it is also the unique symbol of the redemption and transformation of matter, since, of all the Sacraments, it is the only one where the very physical qualities of the material vehicle are transformed, and while the accidents alone remain, the substance, finite and perishable, becomes in an instant of time, and by the Divine miracle of Transubstantiation, infinite and immortal.

I confess that to me the Catholic argument is unanswerable and that only through this doctrine is the philosophy of Christianity rounded out to its fullness. "This is a hard saying: who shall hear it?" and many go back and walk no more with Christ even as in the days when the words were spoken:

> Verily, verily, I say unto you, except ye eat the flesh of the Son of man and drink His blood, ye have no life in you. Whoso eateth my flesh and drinketh my blood, hath eternal life; and I will raise him up at the last day. For my flesh is meat indeed and my blood is drink indeed. He that eateth my flesh and drinketh my blood, dwelleth in me and I in him. As the living Father hath sent me, and I live by the Father: so he that eateth me, even he shall live by me. This is that bread which came down from heaven: not as your fathers did eat manna, and are dead: he that eateth of this bread shall live forever.

We do well to look and work for a new brotherhood of man on earth as the crowning gift of the War: we do better when we pray and labor for the reunion of all Christendom in the One, Holy, Catholic and Apostolic Church, but neither the one nor the other is to be achieved unless to right religion we add a right philosophy. International covenants are ropes of sand, without international love, justice and fidelity, and there is no engine or device of Christian union that will be operative unless it is energized and consecrated by charity—*caritas*—and a consistent, creative, sovereign philosophy of life. If we would have one or both, the Church and the Brotherhood—and both we must have if we are to escape the peril of a new Dark Ages—let us look to it that our religion is redeemed, our philosophy recreated, for otherwise neither individually nor collectively can we meet and turn back the new hordes of Huns and Vandals now gathering for another onslaught on an imperial but futile civilization—no more supreme and irresistible than that other their own kind brought to an end in fire and sack and slaughter just fifteen centuries ago.

I desire to make my plea for the restoration of the one Christian philosophy, in all its integrity and with nothing cut out or cast aside, solely on the ground of its everlasting truth; but even in the acceptance of truth and the establishing of justice there is expediency. As the first step towards a new world-order is a right philosophy—the power "to put things in their right places and control them well" —so it has its bearings on matters that touch us at present very closely, and that must be adjusted without delay if we are to play our part in the new though almost desperate Crusade for the redemption of the Holy Places of the human soul. For the lack of a right philosophy (or of any philosophy whatever, for that matter) the Councillors of the Nations now assembled flounder and fall down, while the nemesis of world-anarchy swiftly overtakes their chaotic deliberations. For the lack of a right philosophy we of *Ecclesia Anglicana* parallel their courses, and have done so time out of mind. The time has come when neither charity nor expediency can permit the Church to continue along the lines of universal comprehension. The Great Testing is at hand, and before that menace of incomparable potency the House of Salvation cannot rest divided against itself. As it is religion alone, the religion of Christ crucified, that can save man at this juncture, so is it the Catholic Church, through its Sacraments and by the strength of its supporting philosophy, that alone can act as the engine of redemptive operation. In the red light of menacing dissolution every predilection, every prejudice, every personal conviction; all except the solemn and unmistakable mandate of conscience alone, must be sacrificed and cast aside. The unity of the Church in the Catholic Faith and under Catholic Authority is the instant and desperate necessity.

To this end the first step is the explicit acceptance of the Catholic doctrine of the Sacraments, and the Catholic philosophy of sacramentalism, with Holy Mass as the true Communion of the true Body and Blood of Christ, as an ever new Sacrifice acceptable before God for the sins of the whole world, and as, in the words of St. Thomas, "the end and aim of all the Sacraments," with Transubstantiation as the sufficient expression of the manner of Christ's Presence therein.

I think it is the lack of this clear consciousness, theologically and philosophically, that is answerable for the vacillating and compromising courses we are disposed to follow, now at this critical moment when we realize that unity in the Church is closely bound up with the great problem whether civilization, even society itself, is to continue except after a second five centuries of Dark Ages. Rightly and honorably we look on the one hand towards the

Protestant denominations, on the other towards all those in Communion with the Apostolic See, tentatively approaching them with well-meant advances, in the desperate hope that so we may have some part in the restoration of Catholic unity. I cannot avoid the conviction that the lack of a definite philosophy has much to do with the variousness of these approaches and the very great unwisdom of some amongst them. A case in point is the question of the acceptance of Episcopal order on the part of those bodies that have rejected it and still protest they desire it not at all. It appears that both in England and America propositions have from time to time been made that practically amount to this: that if the Protestant bodies will only accept the Episcopate as a fact, no questions will be asked as to any theories they may hold as to its nature and function. Now under correction I maintain that this is a case of failing "to put things in their right order and control them well." If the Episcopate represented simply a form of order and government, even with Divine sanction and institution, this might be possible, but in that case I submit we should have no moral right to impose it as an absolute condition, when the question of unity is involved. The doctrine of the Catholic Church is not this, however. The Episcopate has two functions, one of which is the supreme governance of the faithful; but the other and primary function is the transmission to certain men of the Power of the Holy Ghost for the work of a priest in the Church of God, that is to say, first of all for administering the Sacraments of Baptism, Penance, Matrimony and Unction, and, above all, the Communion of the Body and Blood of Christ and the offering of the Holy Sacrifice. In other words, it is not the *fact* of Episcopacy that matters, it is the *function*, and the chief function of the Bishop is the making of priests who can consecrate the Eucharist, forgive sins, and offer the Holy Sacrifice of the Altar.

If then we had a clear and unanimous theological conviction fortified by an equally clear philosophy, we should say to the ministers of those whom we euphemistically call "our separated brethren," not "accept our Bishops and let them have the privilege of ordaining you after their own fashion and we will ask no embarrassing questions as to what you think of it all, or even if you believe you have so gained nothing you did not have before" but rather "You are now a duly accredited 'minister of the Gospel'; do you want to be made a priest? If you do, if you want to act as the agent of God, through the Power of the Holy Ghost to perform the Divine miracle of changing bread and wine into the very Body and Blood of Christ; if you want to gain power for the remitting of sins, and if you want to offer the Holy Sacrifice of the Altar for the quick and the dead and for the sins of the whole world—*then* you will accept the fact and the authority of the Episcopate, and the laying on of hands whereby alone a priest is made by the covenant of God."

So also would it be in the case of laymen, who no longer would "come into the Church" because they had ritualistic leanings, or preferred a different social atmosphere, or for any other of the many causes now operative; they would come because they wanted to confess their sins and receive absolution, because they wanted to feed on Christ Himself through Holy Communion, because they desired to join with the priest in offering the Sacrifice of the Mass for themselves, for their dead, and for the world.

From the lack of a right philosophy our theology is led along divergent lines of strange variation, our order and discipline are weakened to the point of nullity, and even our religion fails of its fullest possibilities, and I know of no way in which *Ecclesia Anglicana* can rise to its vast opportunity at a moment when its peculiar qualities are most needed for the energizing of a true *Vita Nuova*, than by the return to that sacramental philosophy of the Middle Ages which is the only sufficient system and the only intellectually adequate system thus far revealed to man.

From such acceptance, or from the conscious desire for it and progress towards it, will follow of necessity certain acts and ordinances, for every spiritual thing has its material expression. The Mass as the one obligatory service of worship and accepted both as Communion and Sacrifice; formal recognition of marriage as a Sacrament and therefore indissoluble; the restoration of sacramental confession as the normal method of spiritual reconciliation; above all, the establishing of Reservation of the Blessed Sacrament, not only for sick-calls but specifically for private and public adoration, as the recognized custom in every cathedral and parish church. I should perhaps urge the last as the most immediately necessary of all. Where the Sacrament is reserved there is no doubt as to the Catholic faithfulness of priest and people, and as matters rest with us today, it is necessary that the Anglican Church should stand forth from the cowardice and time-serving of an older age to bear witness to the truth of the Incarnation and the Redemption as these are shown forth in the Sacrament of the Body and

Blood of Christ. Not only does the Presence of Christ in the tabernacle transform a church from an echoing conventicle into the very courts of God; not only does it teach mutely but potently as no human voice can do; not only does it lead irresistibly on to the exaltation of the Mass as the one supreme Sacrament and to the other six as of equal authority and obligation; it is also, and for my present purpose most essentially, the explicit, visible teaching of that philosophy which alone can lead men "to put things in their right order and control them well," so perhaps averting from us the nemesis of our own follies and falsities, now increasingly indicated in the Apocalyptic happenings of the world.

I ask then a return, explicit and uncompromising, to that philosophy of life which was the crowning intellectual glory of the great era of the Middle Ages when Christianity was fully operative; to that philosophy which supplemented, in unity and perfection, that Catholic religion that had issue in a righteous and beneficent social system, in a political estate marked by justice and liberty, and in a great and incomparable plexus of all the arts that flowered at last in that Cathedral of Our Lady of Reims which its antithesis, incarnate in modernism, could only desecrate and destroy.

www.ingramcontent.com/pod-product-compliance
Lightning Source LLC
Chambersburg PA
CBHW021157080526
44588CB00008B/388